The Tyndale New Testament Commentaries

General Editor: PROFESSOR R. V. G. TASKER, M.A., B.D.

THE EPISTLES OF PAUL
TO THE THESSALONIANS

THE EPISTLES OF PAUL TO THE

THESSALONIANS

AN INTRODUCTION AND COMMENTARY

by

THE REV. LEON MORRIS

B.Sc., M.Th., Ph.D.

Principal, Ridley College, Melbourne

Inter-Varsity Press,
Leicester, England

William B. Eerdmans Publishing Company
Grand Rapids, Michigan

Inter-Varsity Press
38 De Montfort Street, Leicester LE1 7GP, England
Wm. B. Eerdmans Publishing Company
255 Jefferson S.E., Grand Rapids, MI 49503

First Edition 1958
Reprinted 1983

Published and sold only in the USA and Canada by
Wm. B. Eerdmans Publishing Co.

IVP PAPERBACK EDITION 0 85111 862 3
EERDMANS EDITION 0-8028-1412-3

Printed in the United States of America

*Inter-Varsity Press is the publishing division of the Universities and Colleges
Christian Fellowship (formerly the Inter-Varsity Fellowship), a student move-
ment linking Christian Unions in universities and colleges throughout the
British Isles, and a member movement of the International Fellowship of
Evangelical Students. For information about local and national activities
in Britain write to UCCF, 38 De Montfort Street, Leicester LE1 7GP.*

GENERAL PREFACE

ALL who are interested in the teaching and study of the New Testament today cannot fail to be concerned with the lack of commentaries, written by scholars who are also convinced Christians, which avoid the extremes of being unduly technical or unhelpfully brief. It is the hope of the editor and publishers that this present series will do something towards the supply of this deficiency. Their aim is to place in the hands of students and serious readers of the New Testament, at a moderate cost, commentaries by a number of scholars who, while they are free to make their own individual contributions, are united in a common desire to promote a truly biblical theology.

The commentaries will be primarily exegetical and only secondarily homiletical, though it is hoped that both student and preacher will find them informative and suggestive. Critical questions will be fully considered in introductory sections, and also, at the author's discretion, in additional notes placed at the end of the paragraphs to which they refer.

The commentaries are based on the Authorized (King James) Version, partly because this is the version which most Bible readers possess, and partly because it is easier for commentators, working on this foundation, to show why, on textual and linguistic grounds, the later versions are so often to be preferred. No one translation is regarded as infallible, and no single Greek manuscript or group of manuscripts is regarded as always right! Greek words are transliterated to help those unfamiliar with the language, and to save those who do know Greek the trouble of discovering what word is being discussed.

There are many signs today of a renewed interest in what the Bible has to say and of a more general desire to understand its meaning as fully and clearly as possible. It is the hope of all those concerned with this series that God will graciously use what they have written to further this end.

R. V. G. TASKER.

5

CHIEF ABBREVIATIONS

AV: English Authorized Version (King James).

RV: English Revised Version, 1881.

RSV: American Revised Standard Version, 1946.

Denney: Commentary on 1 & 2 Thessalonians by James Denney in *The Expositor's Bible* (Hodder & Stoughton, 1892).

Findlay (C.B.S.C.): Commentary on 1 & 2 Thessalonians by G. G. Findlay in *The Cambridge Bible for Schools and Colleges*, 1891.

Findlay (C.G.T.): Commentary on 1 & 2 Thessalonians by G. G. Findlay in *The Cambridge Greek Testament*, 1911.

Frame (I.C.C.): Commentary on 1 & 2 Thessalonians by J. E. Frame in *The International Critical Commentary* (T. & T. Clark, 1912).

Lightfoot: *Notes on the Epistles of St. Paul* by J. B. Lightfoot (Macmillan, 1895).

Milligan: Commentary on 1 & 2 Thessalonians by G. Milligan (Macmillan, 1908).

Neil: Commentary on 1 & 2 Thessalonians by William Neil in the *Moffatt New Testament Commentaries*. (Hodder & Stoughton, 1950).

Rutherford: *St. Paul's Epistles to the Thessalonians and to the Corinthians, A New Translation* by the late W. G. Rutherford (Macmillan, 1908).

ACKNOWLEDGEMENTS

Permission to quote from the RSV has been kindly given by the copyright owners, the National Council of the Churches of Christ in the United States of America. Quotations from the Rev. J. B. Phillips' translations of New Testament books are by courtesy of the publishers, Geoffrey Bles Ltd.

CONTENTS

AUTHOR'S PREFACE

THE Epistles to the Thessalonians are all too little studied today. It may be true that they lack the theological profundity of Romans and the exciting controversy of Galatians; but nevertheless their place in Scripture is an important one. No other writing of the great apostle provides a greater insight into his missionary methods and message. Here we see Paul the missionary and Paul the pastor, faithfully proclaiming the gospel of God, concerned for the welfare of his converts, scolding them, praising them, guiding them, exhorting them, teaching them; thrilled with their progress, disappointed with their slowness. Though the continuous exposition of great doctrines is not a characteristic of the Thessalonian writings yet it is fascinating to see how most, if not all, of the great Pauline doctrines are present, either by implication or direct mention. When we consider the undoubtedly early date of these letters this is a fact of importance in the history of Christian thought.

Especially important is the teaching of these Epistles on eschatology; and in view of the revival of interest in this doctrine in recent times it is imperative that we understand and appreciate the contribution of Thessalonians to this difficult subject. It is my earnest hope that this short commentary may help to direct the attention of Christian people to the importance of these Epistles and the relevance of their message for the men of today.

Every commentator, I suppose, bases his work on that of his predecessors, and in this I am certainly no exception. I have learned much from those who have written on these Epistles before me, and cannot hope to have acknowledged all my indebtednesses. I have found particularly helpful the commentaries by Milligan, Frame (I.C.C.), Denney (*Expositor's Bible*), Findlay (who wrote two commentaries, one in the *Cambridge Bible for Schools and Colleges*, and the other in the *Cambridge Greek Testament* series), and Neil (*Moffatt New Testament Commentary*), while Lightfoot's *Notes on the Epistles of St. Paul* is a veritable treasure-house.

Finally may I express my indebtedness to a number of my friends who have interested themselves in this project and made helpful suggestions. Especially am I indebted to the Very Rev. Dr. S. Barton Babbage, the Rev. David Livingstone, and Mr. I. Siggins, who read the typescript, and suggested many improvements.

LEON MORRIS.

INTRODUCTION

I. BACKGROUND

IN the first century A.D. Thessalonica was the capital of Macedonia, and its largest city. The geographical importance of its site may be gauged from the fact that the modern Salonika is still an important town. It is usually said that the name of the city in earlier days was Therma (from its hot springs), and that c. 315 B.C. it was renamed by Cassander after his wife Thessalonica, half-sister to Alexander the Great. But as the elder Pliny refers to Therma and Thessalonica as existing together,[1] it would seem that Cassander founded a new town, which in due course extended and swallowed up the more ancient one nearby. Under the Romans it was the capital of the second of the four divisions of Macedonia, and when these were united to form one single province in 146 B.C. it became the capital, as well as the largest city of the province. Thessalonica was a free city, and inscriptions confirm the accuracy of Luke in calling its rulers 'politarchs'. It was strategically situated on the Via Egnatia, the great Roman highway to the East.

To this city came Paul in company with Silas and Timothy. The former was Paul's partner on his second missionary journey, chosen after the great apostle had separated from Barnabas. We first read of him when he and Judas Barsabas, 'chief men among the brethren' (Acts xv. 22), and 'prophets' (Acts xv. 32), were sent to Antioch after the council of Jerusalem to convey to the believers there, both by letter and by word of mouth, the decisions which the council had taken. He accompanied Paul on that apostle's second missionary journey, and Paul makes approving mention of his preaching (2 Cor. i. 19). In later times we read of him as associated with Peter in the writing of the First Epistle of Peter (1 Pet. v. 12). It is interesting that Paul and Peter both use the longer and

[1] *N.H.*, IV, 17.

more formal name Silvanus, while Luke employs the shorter form, the nickname Silas.

Timothy first comes under notice when Paul met him at Lystra and had him circumcised as a preliminary to his accompanying the apostle for the remainder of his second missionary journey. He became closely associated with Paul, as we see from the joint salutations in 2 Corinthians, Colossians, 1 and 2 Thessalonians and Philemon. From 1 Cor. xvi. 10 and the general tone of references to him, we gather that Timothy was somewhat timid in disposition. But he was high in Paul's confidence, for Paul sent him on missions (Acts xix. 22; 1 Cor. iv. 17; Phil. ii. 19), and could link his preaching with his own (2 Cor. i. 19). Paul speaks warmly of his attitude to those to whom he ministered and to himself (Phil. ii. 20–22).

The three men had previously preached at Philippi, but had been compelled to leave after the imprisonment of Paul and Silas (Acts xvi). They then came to Thessalonica, where Paul followed his usual practice of going to the synagogue. He preached there on three (apparently successive) sabbaths (Acts xvii. 2), with some success. His converts included some Jews, 'a great multitude' of devout Greeks, and 'not a few' of the chief women (Acts xvii. 4).[1] The chief success of the mission clearly lay among those Greeks who had attached themselves to the synagogue. People of this type were dissatisfied with the low standards of pagan morality and with the idol worship which fostered them. They were attracted by the monotheism and lofty morality of Judaism, but, at the same time, were repelled by its narrow nationalism and ritual requirements. In Christianity they found a faith that satisfied. Some of the converts came of high class families, but it is probable that most were from the lower classes, for Paul stressed his refusal to be dependent on them in any way (1 Thes. ii. 9), and in his letters there are no warnings about the dangers attendant on riches.

[1]This harmonizes with the fact that in Macedonia women had rather more liberty than elsewhere. See Lightfoot on Philippians, pp. 55–7; W. Ramsay, *St. Paul the Traveller and the Roman Citizen*, London, 1940, p. 227.

The Jewish community did not take kindly to losing a considerable section of their adherents. They therefore resorted to violence, inciting the rabble to make an attack on the house of Jason, Paul's host (Acts xvii. 5). The mob took Jason before the politarchs, complaining that he had lodged those who 'have turned the world upside down' (Acts xvii. 6), and that the preachers had acted contrary to Caesar's laws in declaring Jesus to be another king (Acts xvii. 7). This is the first record of such an accusation since Jesus was brought before Pilate. The conception of Christ reigning may refer to Paul's preaching of the second coming, which would accord with what we read in our Epistles. The politarchs took security of Jason and some others unnamed, and let them go.

It is not clear to what Jason and the others were bound. T. W. Manson thinks it was 'not to harbour seditious persons';[1] and others write similarly, though we should notice that this goes beyond the statement of Acts. K. and S. Lake think of Paul as having in effect 'jumped his bail'[2] when he left the city, but this is pure assumption. Frame is of the opinion that the security had nothing to do with Paul's absence, since the converts were surprised at his failure to return.[3] But the evidence for this surprise does not seem at all adequate. It is clear, however, that Paul did envisage a return (1 Thes. ii. 17f.), so it seems impossible that Jason undertook that he would stay away. Our best conjecture is that Jason and the other Christians were bound over to keep the peace, and that, in the troubled state of the moment, all were agreed that it would be better for Paul and Silas to leave immediately, at least for a time.

From Thessalonica they proceeded to Beroea, where their preaching was successful until Thessalonian Jews followed them, and stirred up such opposition that Paul was compelled to leave, upon which he journeyed to Athens (Acts xvii. 13f.). From there he sent word to Silas and Timothy asking them to rejoin him, and then gave himself over to the preaching which

---

[1]*Bull. Ryl. Lib.*, March 1953, p. 432.
[2]*An Introduction to the New Testament*, London, 1938, p. 135.
[3]I.C.C., p. 4.

led to his Areopagite address and his subsequent departure from the city, having apparently accomplished but little. He went on to Corinth, and was presently joined by Silas and Timothy there (Acts xviii. 5). But from 1 Thes. iii. 2 it is clear that Timothy had previously joined Paul at Athens and then had been sent back to Thessalonica. It was on his return from this second visit to the city that he joined Paul at Corinth.

Up to this point Paul had had little to encourage him. In four successive centres there had been discouragement. A promising beginning had been followed by forcible disruption in Philippi, Thessalonica and Beroea, and in Athens he had had little success. Small wonder that he began his preaching at Corinth 'in weakness, and in fear, and in much trembling' (1 Cor. ii. 3). But when the messengers came from Thessalonica they brought such a report of the continuing stedfastness of the converts that Paul saw that the blessing of God had after all rested upon his work there, and this so caused his spirits to rise that he was able to give himself much more energetically to the work he was doing. This appears to be the meaning of 'Paul was pressed in the spirit, and testified to the Jews that Jesus was Christ' (Acts xviii. 5). Out of this sense of relief and reassurance Paul wrote his first letter to the Thessalonians, and it is clear that he wrote with a full heart.

There are some later contacts with this church. We read of Paul sending Timothy to Macedonia (Acts xix. 22), while he himself made two visits to the same region (Acts xx. 1–3). Some of the Thessalonians became his travelling companions, for example Aristarchus (Acts xix. 29, xx. 4, xxvii. 2), Secundus (Acts xx. 4) and perhaps Demas (Phm. 24; 2 Tim. iv. 10).

II. DATE OF COMPOSITION OF I THESSALONIANS

This Epistle was clearly written not long after Timothy came to Paul (1 Thes. iii. 6, cf. ii. 17). This meeting may have been the one which took place in Athens (see 1 Thes. iii. 1f.), but is more probably the one which took place at Corinth (see Acts xviii. 5), for the longer period seems necessary for the situation in Thessalonica to develop to the point where advice of the kind given was necessary. The longer period seems also to agree better with the fact that, by the time the letter was written, the faith of the Thessalonians was spoken of 'in every place' (1 Thes. i. 8).

While Paul was in Corinth he was arrested and brought before Gallio, the proconsul of Achaia. Now an inscription at Delphi, dealing with a question referred to the Emperor Claudius by this same Gallio, is dated in the twelfth year of the Emperor's tribunicial power and after his twenty-sixth acclamation as Emperor. This twelfth year was from 25th January 52 to 24th January 53; also, while the date of the twenty-sixth acclamation is not exactly known, the twenty-seventh was before 1st August 52. Thus Claudius' decision would have been given to Gallio during the first half of 52. Now proconsuls usually took office in early summer and held office for one year. It would seem, therefore, that Gallio entered his term of office in the early summer of 51, for there hardly seems time for him to refer a matter to Rome and have the decision given if he was not appointed until 52.

Our difficulties are that, while we know that Paul was in Corinth for eighteen months (Acts xviii. 11), we do not know at what point in the eighteen months he appeared before the proconsul, nor at what stage of Gallio's proconsulship this took place, nor whether Gallio may, exceptionally, have had a second year in office. The impression we gather from Acts xviii. 12–18 is that it was early in Gallio's term of office, and towards the end (though not right at the end) of Paul's eighteen months. If this is so, then Paul arrived in Corinth in the early part of 50, and 1 Thessalonians would have been written soon after. But in view of the uncertainties attaching to the question we can regard this date as approximate only.[1] But it is clear that the letters to the Thessalonians are among the earliest of the New Testament documents. Galatians may have been written earlier, but no other of Paul's letters.

[1]The inscription and other relevant texts are quoted and discussed by Kirsopp Lake in *The Beginnings of Christianity*, Vol. v, London, 1933, pp. 46off.

III. THE AUTHENTICITY OF I THESSALONIANS

The authenticity of 1 Thessalonians has not been seriously doubted other than by the Tübingen school, and the objections they raised have failed to stand the test of time. It is included in Marcion's canon (c. A.D. 140), is mentioned in the Muratorian Fragment (giving the list of books accepted as Scripture, probably at Rome some time after the middle of the second century), and is quoted by name by Irenaeus (c. A.D. 180), after which it is universally accepted. The contents are all in favour of its being genuine. It is obviously early, for the organization of the Church appears to be rudimentary; an answer to the problem of what would happen to those who died before the Parousia must have been given early; and it is difficult to imagine a later writer ascribing to Paul after his death statements which might be interpreted as meaning that the Parousia would occur during his lifetime. The language and ideas are Pauline.

If the letter is not from Paul it is hard to imagine a reason for its composition. There seems no motive for forgery. Indeed, it has been said that the best argument for its authenticity is the letter itself. 'What is its point if it is not a genuine message from the apostle to a church he has founded and a people whom he loved?'[1] The existence of 2 Thessalonians, whatever its date, seems to imply the existence and the acceptance of 1 Thessalonians.[2]

For reasons such as these practically all accept the Epistle as a genuine writing of the apostle Paul. It is sometimes alleged, however, that there are serious discrepancies with Acts, and we must now examine these.[3]

1. Acts xvii. 2 speaks of Paul reasoning in the synagogue

---

[1]Neil, p. xviii.

[2]W. Lock regards this as the 'strongest support' of the authenticity of 1 Thessalonians (H.D.B., IV, p. 745). A. Plummer speaks similarly in *A Commentary on St. Paul's First Epistle to the Thessalonians*, London, 1918, p. xi.

[3]Of the attitude of some critics Moffatt says, 'It is capricious to pronounce the epistle a colourless imitation, if it agrees with Acts, and unauthentic if it disagrees' (*An Introduction to the Literature of the New Testament*, Edinburgh, 1927, p. 71).

three sabbaths, whereas I Thes. ii. 7–11 shows Paul working at his trade. This seems to imply a longer period of residence, and this is supported by Phil. iv. 16, which is usually held to mean that the Philippians twice sent him gifts while he was at Thessalonica.

There is no contradiction here. Clearly Paul's visit was in the nature of an evangelistic campaign, and he did not have time to build up the church as he would have wished, so that the period must have been short.[1] Even if he was there for only about a month it is likely that he would have to work for his living (not everyone can afford a month without income); and it is not beyond the bounds of possibility, though admittedly not very likely, that within that period the friends from Philippi helped him twice. But Phil. iv. 16 probably does not mean that help was sent to Paul twice while he was in Thessalonica. *Hapax kai dis* appears to mean 'more than once', and with *kai* prefixed it will signify, 'both (when I was) in Thessalonica and (*kai*) more than once (*hapax kai dis*) (when I was in other places) you sent . . . '.[2] Even if Acts gives the total duration of the stay there is no contradiction.

But it is not certain that it does. Acts may well be concerned only with the time spent on the Jewish mission, and there is nothing in the narrative to exclude a further period among the Gentiles. Ramsay is of the opinion that the most likely reading of the evidence is that the stay in Thessalonica lasted about six months.[3]

2. In Acts xvii. 4 the converts are both Jews and Gentiles, but I Thes. i. 9, ii. 14 refer to Gentiles, and the mention of turning from idols shows that former pagans rather than the devout who attached themselves to the synagogues are in mind. This, however, seems to show only that there were

[1] Cf. Lake, 'the suggestion of a more prolonged preaching in Thessalonica seems psychologically as unnecessary as it is certainly historically unvouched for' (*The Earlier Epistles of St. Paul*, London, 1919, p. 65).

[2] Frame (on I Thes. ii. 18) differs from this view of Phil. iv. 16 only in that he understands *hapax kai dis* to mean the slightly stronger 'repeatedly'.

[3] *Op. cit.*, p. 228. Findlay thinks that this is 'perhaps an extreme view' (C.G.T., p. xx, n.) but he thinks the duration of the mission to have been months, rather than weeks.

various strata represented among the converts, and that the accounts are independent.

3. Acts xviii. 5 speaks of Silas and Timothy rejoining Paul at Corinth, but 1 Thes. iii. 1f. shows that Timothy was with Paul in Athens. This simply means that neither is giving a full report. Clearly Timothy came to Athens, from which place Paul sent him to Thessalonica and in due course he rejoined Paul at Corinth, in company with Silas.

As Clogg says 'Discrepancies of this nature prove little except that the authors of Acts and of 1 Thessalonians wrote independently of each other.'[1]

IV. PURPOSE OF I THESSALONIANS

The coming of the messengers from Thessalonica was a source of much encouragement to Paul, and we have already noted that he wrote to help the young church they had left behind. The principal points which called for attention seem to have been the following.

1. The Jewish opponents of the Christian way were maintaining a campaign in which a principal element seems to have been slander of St. Paul. If they could have succeeded in demonstrating that his conduct was dishonourable they might well have made it very difficult for his converts to hold their ground. They appear to have insinuated that Paul's concern was to make a profit out of them, like some of the wandering teachers (of philosophy or religion) who abounded at this time. So, too, they apparently made capital out of his failure to return, alleging that it showed him to have no real love for them. They probably suggested that there was nothing divine about Paul's message, and that it had originated in the apostle's own fertile mind. It is clear that Paul is answering allegations of this kind throughout his first three chapters, and the fact that he thought it necessary to devote this amount of space to these slanders may indicate that the whispering campaign was having some measure of success.

2. There was persecution by the pagans (ii. 14f.).

[1] *An Introduction to the New Testament*, London, 1940, p. 21.

3. In a pagan environment pressure was always being exerted on those newly converted from paganism to revert to easy-going pagan standards in sexual matters (iv. 4ff.).

4. Some of the Christians had apparently understood Paul to have said that Christ would come back and receive them all to Himself. When some of them died they thought this meant that they would lose their share in the glory attendant on the Parousia (iv. 13ff.).

5. It is possible that some were worried about when the Parousia would take place (v. 1ff.).

6. Some of the brethren seem to have been content to live on their fellows, instead of earning their own living (iv. 11f.).

7. A tension may well have been present between some of the leading members and the rest of the congregation (v. 12f.).

8. There may have been some difficulty about the work of the Holy Spirit and the importance to be attached to spiritual gifts (v. 19f.).

Much of this is explicable as the difficulties which a young, very enthusiastic, but as yet imperfectly instructed, church would naturally encounter as it sought to live out its faith. We meet the weak and the faint-hearted, the idlers and the workers, the visionaries and the puzzled.

So Paul the pastor wrote to meet the need of his flock. It is clear enough that, on the whole, he was well satisfied with the progress the Thessalonians had made; indeed the news brought to him had thrilled him. But he was never the man to dwell on past achievements, whether his own or those of his converts. Thus he applies himself at once to the task of meeting the needs that had been revealed. The result is a moving document; and while it is true that many of the important Pauline doctrines are absent, it is also true that the letter reveals to us something of Paul's pastoral zeal and his intense interest in the spiritual well-being of his converts. Here we catch a glimpse of Paul the man in a way we do not always do when he is taken up with questions of more profound theological significance.

V. THE AUTHENTICITY OF II THESSALONIANS

The authenticity of this Epistle seems to rest on such considerations as the following:

1. 2 Thessalonians is, if anything, better attested than the first Epistle. Polycarp, Ignatius and Justin all seem to have known it; it is included in the Marcionite canon and the Muratorian Fragment; Irenaeus quotes it by name; and from then onwards it is universally accepted.

2. The vocabulary, style and basic theology are as Pauline as those in 1 Thessalonians.

3. The general situation presupposed, and the contents are in agreement with what we might expect if Paul were the author.

4. There seems no suitable alternative. If Paul did not write the letter, we must suppose that a forger did. We cannot dismiss it as well-intentioned writing under the general coverage of the apostle's name, for 2 Thes. iii. 17 claims to be Paul's authentic signature. But this being so, what possible motive could the forger have had? Unless the letter is written to meet the genuine need of the Thessalonian church there seems no point in it. Nor can we understand why he should make it so like 1 Thessalonians, or for that matter how he did it. He must have entered very fully into the apostle's mind.

5. Finally, there is von Dobschutz's point that the only reason for doubting the authenticity of 2 Thessalonians is that we possess 1 Thessalonians. It is strange procedure to reject an Epistle which contains nothing un-Pauline, and bears all the marks of a Pauline utterance, simply because we have another Pauline utterance which is markedly similar.

But despite such considerations there have been serious doubts raised about it; and many scholars are hesitant, although few would go so far as to pronounce it unauthentic. The following seem to be the more important objections:

(a) Eschatology

The eschatology is said to be inconsistent with that of 1 Thessalonians. The point is urged that in the first Epistle the

Parousia is thought of as imminent and as something which will occur suddenly, whereas in the second it is to be preceded by signs, notably the appearance of the Man of Lawlessness. It is difficult to take this argument seriously, for it demands a logical consistency which is foreign to the very nature of apocalyptic. Most apocalypses manage to hold to the two ideas of suddenness and the appearance of preparatory signs. Again, the fact that in 1 Thes. v. 1–11 Paul exhorts his readers not to let the Parousia catch them unprepared might well be held to imply that they had such knowledge of the signs as 2 Thessalonians assumes.

Another criticism similar to the above affirms that 2 Thessalonians contains a view of the anti-Christ without parallel in the New Testament, and therefore we cannot ascribe it to Paul. But this is a palpable *non sequitur*. If it is unique, that is no reason for denying it to Paul. His ideas were not commonly those which any one in the Early Church could have produced.

Another way of putting the objection from eschatology is to ask whether readers who knew all about the anti-Christ (as is shown by the manner of reference in the second Epistle) could possibly be ignorant of the matters which have to be explained in 1 Thes. iv. 13ff. But it is clear that Paul did not have sufficient time in Thessalonica to give all the teaching he would have liked, and it is quite possible that some of his converts received enthusiastically enough his general teaching on the Parousia, including the appearance of the anti-Christ, without getting to grips with the problem of those who died before the Parousia. Indeed this is a problem which might well have suggested itself only when some of the Thessalonian believers died.

Yet another criticism along these lines is that which sees in the section on the anti-Christ a reference to the Nero *redivivus*, myth. Nero died in 68, but in the following year an impostor appeared giving out that he was Nero. He was speedily destroyed, but others appeared in subsequent years. Eventually Nero's death became accepted, but the expectation continued that he would come back to life again, and lead a force opposed to all that is good. The picture came to have a supernatural tinge, so that Nero was thought of as in a sense human, and in another sense demon.

Now, clearly, if this is the source of the reference to the Man of Sin, Paul could not be the author, for it was years after his death before the Nero *redivivus* myth began to spread abroad. But Bousset has shown that the idea of the anti-Christ is far older than the Nero *redivivus* conception, and that it can be traced to a time before that of Paul. Writing in 1919 Kirsopp Lake could say: 'the result of the last fifteen years of research is decisively to remove the eschatological argument from the list of possible objections to the authenticity of 2 Thessalonians',[1] and nothing has happened in the intervening years to alter this verdict. The difference in eschatology between the two Epistles is one of emphasis, not principle. As Clogg puts it: 'it is reasonable to suppose that the Apostle is correcting a misapprehension, or possibly a wilful misrepresentation, of the eschatology of the first letter, rather than that he is correcting the eschatology itself'.[2]

(b) *The combination of likeness and difference*

The main argument against the authenticity of this letter is the problem of accounting for the combination of likeness to and difference from 1 Thessalonians. On the one hand there is the fact that large sections of the two Epistles are very similar, not simply in ideas, but in the actual phraseology used. Would a writer of the calibre of Paul repeat himself in this way after such a short interval when writing to the same people?

---

[1]*Op. cit.*, p. 80. Baur, who decisively rejected the Pauline authorship of both Epistles, could yet say: 'It is perfectly conceivable that one and the same writer, if he lived so much in the thought of the Parousia as the two Epistles testify, should have looked at this mysterious subject in different circumstances and from different points of view, and so expressed himself regarding it in different ways' (quoted in Maurice Jones, *The New Testament in the Twentieth Century*, London, 1934, pp. 266f.).

[2]*Op. cit.*, p. 25. G. G. Findlay thinks that, since 2 Thessalonians 'is written on purpose to qualify the former and to correct an erroneous inference that might be drawn from it . . . a *prima facie* disagreement on the point is only to be expected' (*op. cit.*, p. lii).

Deliberate imitation by another, rather than a second missive from the same pen, is said to be the explanation. On the other hand there are the differences such as those noticed in the previous section. It is difficult to imagine circumstances which would explain this combination of likeness and difference, and thus some feel that it is better to think of 2 Thessalonians as being written by someone other than Paul who tried to gain acceptance for it by passing it off as the product of the great apostle.

Of this we might say, in the first place, that some of the resemblances are such that it is very difficult to think of the author being other than Paul. As we have seen already, the style, vocabulary, and ideas are all Pauline, and a forger would have to be imbued with the very mind of Paul to have produced such a work. Deliberate imitation is not the only explanation of the language coincidences; for example, it is not impossible that Paul may have refreshed his memory by looking over a copy of 1 Thessalonians. (Neil is of this opinion, though Milligan scouts the idea.)

Again, the extent of the resemblances should not be exaggerated. If we exclude the framework of the Epistles (opening, closing, etc.), the resemblances do not occur in more than about one-third. Moreover, passages with similar wording are used differently in the two letters. For example, the reference to Paul's working with his hands comes early in the first Epistle, and shows Paul's love for his converts (1 Thes. ii. 9); but in the second it is late, and is the basis of an exhortation to imitate the apostle (2 Thes. iii. 7f.).[1]

Of the differences, those connected with the eschatological teaching are the most serious. But, as we have seen, they raise no insuperable barrier to common authorship.

The verdict of Lake may be used to sum up this section: 'The main argument against the Epistle is the difficulty of imagining circumstances to account for its curious combination

---

[1]Frame thinks that, 'Apart from the epistolary outline, the agreements are seldom lengthy. Furthermore, the setting of the phrases in II is usually different from their setting in I' (*op. cit.*, p. 49).

of likeness to and difference from the first Epistle—and such an argument is too negative to be ever quite decisive'.[1]

(c) Difference in tone

The general tone of 2 Thessalonians is said to be colder and more formal than that of the first Epistle. This objection can be answered in a number of ways. In the first place we might ask why a second letter should precisely reproduce the tone of the first,[2] especially when the first was evidently written in a time of exaltation, when Paul was reacting from extreme discouragement. Indeed, since it is clear that some of the rebukes given in the first Epistle have to be repeated in the second, it should not surprise us if a tone of asperity were to creep in. This is all the more important in that it appears from 2 Thes. iii. 2 that Paul's circumstances were not happy at the time he wrote.

But we may well doubt whether the difference in tone is as pronounced as is alleged. It depends on a few expressions such as 'We are bound to thank God always for you, brethren, as it is meet' (2 Thes. i. 3, and cf. ii. 13), 'we command you' (2 Thes. iii. 6, and iii. 12). But there seems little that is formal or cold in the way Paul deals with the offenders. Moreover, if we look again at the first Epistle we see that most of the colour comes in the section where Paul is defending himself against the slanderers (ii. 1–13): for the rest there is little difference in tone between the two. As Frame says, 'Omit the self-defence from I and the differences in tone between I and II would not be perceptible'.[3]

Thus, because none of the considerations which are urged against the authenticity of the Epistle can be held to be

[1] *Op. cit.*, p. 86.

[2] 'We are not called upon to assume that Paul at all times lived in the same mood of emotional exaltation . . . it is unreasonable to expect him always to write in the same key' (R. H. Walker, *The International Standard Bible Encyclopaedia*, v, p. 2969). Similarly Findlay reports Bornemann's view that, by the time of 2 Thessalonians, 'St. Paul was immersed in Corinthian affairs . . . his heart was no longer away at Thessalonica as when he first wrote' (*op. cit.*, p. xlix).

[3] *Op. cit.*, p. 35.

decisive, and in view of the positive evidence in its favour, we conclude that this is a genuine Epistle of Paul.

VI. THE RELATION BETWEEN THE TWO EPISTLES

The considerations in favour of the authenticity of 2 Thessalonians seem very strong indeed, but they do not settle the question of the relationship between the two Epistles. In connection with this various alternatives have been suggested.

(a) A church in two sections

Harnack envisaged the Jews and the Gentiles in the church at Thessalonica as being sufficiently out of step with each other as to be meeting separately, and he thought that, while 1 Thessalonians is addressed to the Gentile section of the church, 2 Thessalonians is meant for the Jewish section. He pointed out that, whereas the first Epistle seems addressed to Gentiles (cf. the reference to turning to God from idols in 1 Thes. i. 9), there is a marked Jewish colouring in the second Epistle which points to a different public, and one familiar with Old Testament phraseology. This does not amount to very much, for Paul's most copious use of the Old Testament is in the Epistle to the Romans, a church which was predominantly Gentile. Moreover, the Jewish tone of 2 Thessalonians is not very clear. There is not one direct quotation from the Old Testament, and Plummer, who has searched both Epistles for traces of LXX phraseology, finds this 'less conspicuous' in the second than in the first.[1]

A second point is based upon a variant reading in 2 Thes. ii. 13, where the usual text reads 'God hath from the beginning (*ap' archēs*) chosen you', while the variant substitutes 'a first

---

[1] *A Commentary on St. Paul's Second Epistle to the Thessalonians*, London, 1918, p. xviiff. G. Milligan, however, finds 2 Thes. i. 6–10 the best illustration of his contention that in these two Epistles 'there are whole passages which are little more than a mosaic of O.T. words and expressions' (*op. cit.*, pp. lviiif.), while G. G. Findlay thinks the mind of the writer of 2 Thessalonians to be 'full of the apocalyptic ideas of the Books of Isaiah and Daniel, to a less extent of Ezekiel and the Psalter' and 'his prophetical and hortatory passages are so steeped in the O.T., beyond what is common with St. Paul, that this fact is even urged as evidence for inauthenticity' (*op. cit.*, p. lx).

fruit' (*aparchēn*) for 'from the beginning'. The variant has sufficiently strong manuscript support for Lake to say 'there is about as much to be said for the one reading as the other'.[1] If it be accepted, it supports Harnack's view, for, while the Thessalonians were not in any sense a first fruit (being neither Paul's first converts, nor the first in Macedonia), the Jewish Christians were the first fruits of the Thessalonian church.

Then there is the 'all' of 1 Thes. v. 26f. It is felt that there must be something behind the insistence that *all* the brethren should be greeted, and that the letter be read to *all*. This solution attracted Lake,[2] but there seem to be insuperable difficulties.

1. It is incredible that the man who wrote 1 Cor. i. 11ff. should meekly have acquiesced in a situation where a church of his foundation was so hopelessly rent. The idea is at variance with his repeated stress on unity.

2. It is difficult to explain Paul's evident pleasure in the Thessalonians if such a split were in existence.

3. The division of a church into two communities of this type is so contradictory to all that we know of apostolic Christianity that we could accept it only on the basis of very strong evidence.

4. Even if there were a split church anywhere, the evidence that the church in Thessalonica was so divided is very weak, to put it mildly.

5. The superscriptions of the two Epistles are practically identical, and there is not the slightest indication that they are addressed to different groups. Harnack has to suppose that 'which are of the circumcision' has dropped out of the text in the second Epistle.

6. 1 Thes. ii. 13–16, which would on this hypothesis be intended for the Gentile section of the church, holds up for admiration the conduct of the churches in Judæa, and commends the Thessalonians for following this example.

[1] *Op. cit.*, p. 84.
[2] *Op. cit.*, p. 83ff., and this position is still maintained in *An Introduction to the New Testament*, London, 1938, p. 134.

Moreover there are traces of LXX phraseology behind some of the language of the first Epistle.[1]

7. Each of the points adduced in favour of the hypothesis may fairly be disputed. We have already noted that the more Jewish tone of 2 Thessalonians is difficult to sustain; the variant reading does not carry conviction; while the 'all' of 1 Thes. v. 26f. is not particularly emphatic and is accounted for by Paul's desire to send his greetings to everybody (see the notes).

(b) Co-authorship

Some have felt that the best solution is to think of Silas[2] or Timothy[3] as the real author of one or both of the Epistles, with Paul simply adding a general authentication. But this really solves nothing. If, with Burkitt, we think of the same man as being the author of both Epistles we are faced with exactly the same problems as when we think of Paul as being the author of both. If we think of Paul as the author of the first Epistle and of Timothy or Silas as the author of the second we are faced with the problem of the style and language, which are the same in both. Nor is this theory any better when it comes to explaining the differences between the two, for Paul clearly signed 2 Thessalonians (2 Thes. iii. 17) and we cannot imagine him putting his signature to something with which he disagreed.

(c) Reversal of order

We have hitherto assumed that 1 Thessalonians was written first and 2 Thessalonians after a short interval. But some scholars have felt that many of the difficulties are solved if we

[1]Plummer finds evidence of LXX phraseology behind six or seven passages in this Epistle. *A Commentary on St. Paul's First Epistle to the Thessalonians*, London, 1918, pp. xxff.

[2]Burkitt thought that both letters 'were drafted by Silvanus-Silas, that they were read to Paul, who approved them and added 1 Thes. ii. 18 and 2 Thes. iii. 17 with his own hand' (quoted in *The New Bible Commentary*, Ed. F. Davidson, A. M. Stibbs, E. F. Kevan, London, 1954, p. 1059).

[3]W. Lock cites Spitta as holding this view. He thinks Silas more likely than Timothy, 'but the theory creates more difficulties than it solves' (H. D. B., IV, p. 748). Milligan examines this view but finds against it 'the want ... of any satisfactory direct evidence' (*op. cit.*, p. xc).

reverse the order. The reason for thinking 2 Thessalonians unauthentic, they would say, is that we read it in the shadow of 1 Thessalonians, and beside that letter it does appear as something in the nature of a pale copy. But, as a first letter, it is full of life and interest, though it leaves some things unsettled, and thus calls for the fuller letter to follow.

The case has been cogently argued by T. W. Manson,[1] who cites with approval various points made by Johannes Weiss:

1. The trials and tribulations mentioned are at their height in 2 Thessalonians, but are spoken of as past in 1 Thessalonians.

2. In 2 Thessalonians the internal difficulties are spoken of as a new development of which the writers of the letter have just heard, whereas in 1 Thessalonians they are referred to as completely familiar to all concerned.

3. The statement that the Thessalonians have no need to be instructed about times and seasons (1 Thes. v. 1) is very relevant if they are acquainted with 2 Thes. ii.

To these Manson adds:

4. The formula 'Now concerning. . . .' in 1 Thes. iv. 9, 13, v. 1, is like that in 1 Cor. vii. 1 and elsewhere, where the writer is replying to points raised in a letter sent to him. Manson thinks that the replies may well be to certain questions arising from statements in 2 Thessalonians.[2]

None of these is really convincing. It is by no means clear from 1 Thessalonians that the trials are over and, indeed, most students have felt that part, at least, of the purpose of that Epistle is to encourage the brethren in view of the difficulties ahead. The idea that the internal difficulties mentioned are a new development in 2 Thessalonians seems to rest mainly on the 'For we hear that there are some' of 2 Thes. iii. 11, which is just as compatible with a report reaching Paul after 1 Thessalonians as before it. Otherwise the

---

[1] *Bull. Ryl. Lib.*, March, 1953 pp. 438ff.

[2] But cf. Plummer: 'it is not difficult to construct a series of questions to which portions of 1 Thessalonians might be an answer. A similar letter of inquiry might be constructed to fit Philippians, but it would go very little way towards proving that any such letter had been written' (*op. cit.*, pp. xviiif.).

injunctions in the second letter are very similar to those in the first. The statement about the autograph as a mark of genuineness seems adequately explained from 2 Thes. ii. 2 which makes it clear that they needed some criterion to discern a genuine Pauline letter from one which was spurious. But that it was not a necessary part of a first letter is shown by the fact that it does not occur elsewhere in the Pauline correspondence.[1]

We have already noted that there is nothing in the eschatology of 2 Thessalonians which is incompatible with that of the first Epistle, while Manson's last point, though interesting, is by no means conclusive, and could well refer to matters mentioned by Timothy in his report on the situation in Thessalonica.

Against this position we may note:

1. Each of the problems occupying Paul's attention—persecution, the Parousia, idleness—seems to intensify and deepen as we pass from the first to the second Epistle.

2. There are passages in 2 Thessalonians which refer to a letter from Paul (see ii. 2, 15, iii. 17). Unless we take these as pointing us to 1 Thessalonians we must postulate some lost Epistle.

3. The personal reminiscences which form so prominent a part of the first letter are lacking in the second, which is perfectly natural if the latter is something in the nature of a sequel to the first, but not so natural if it was a first missive. So conclusive did this seem to Milligan that he could say that the idea of the priority of 2 Thessalonians 'is excluded by I. ii. 17—iii. 6 which could hardly have been written by St. Paul, if he had previously addressed a letter to Thessalonica'.[2]

---

[1] The autograph occurs in 1 Cor. xvi. 21 and Col. iv. 18, but no attention is drawn to it in either case, as is done in 2 Thes. iii. 17.

[2] *Op. cit.*, p. xxxix. Cf. B. Jowett: 'It is improbable (observe, however, 2 Thes. ii. 15) that a previous Epistle could have interposed itself between the visit of the Apostle and chapters two and three of the First Epistle. (Compare Acts xvii, xviii.)' *The Epistles of St. Paul to the Thessalonians, Galatians and Romans*, London, 1894, Vol. 1, p. 67.

4. We have seen that the warmth of the expressions in the first letter spring naturally out of the news of their situation which Timothy brought, while the slightly cooler tone of 2 Thessalonians is natural later on. It is difficult to reverse the situation. Thus it would seem that there are no sufficient grounds for thinking that the usual order of these Epistles is anything but the right one.

VII. THE OCCASION AND PURPOSE OF II THESSALONIANS

The situation, then, would seem to be that Paul wrote 1 Thessalonians, but that it did not achieve all that he desired. Further reports reaching him showed that his defence of his own conduct had proved adequate (this we may gather from the fact that he did not repeat it), but apparently other parts of his letter were not so effective. Idleness on the part of some continued, and there were misunderstandings about the Parousia which caused others to be troubled in mind. Accordingly, without losing time (by common consent there cannot have been more than a matter of weeks between the two Epistles), Paul set himself to the task of putting things in order, and 2 Thessalonians is the result. It must have been written soon after 1 Thessalonians, because it must have been sent prior to Paul's second visit to Thessalonica (see Acts xx. 1f.), and Corinth is the only place known to us where Paul, Silas and Timothy were together during the intervening period.

In this second letter he carries on the work of the first, encouraging the faint hearted, rebuking the slackers, clearing up points associated with the return of the Lord. 'It is simply a second prescription for the same case, made after discovering that certain stubborn symptoms had not yielded to the first treatment.'[1]

[1] R. H. Walker, in *The International Standard Bible Encyclopaedia*, v, p. 2968.

I THESSALONIANS: ANALYSIS

I. GREETING, i. 1.

II. PRAYER OF THANKSGIVING, i. 2–4.

III. REMINISCENCES, i. 5—ii. 16.
   (a) Response of the Thessalonians to the original preaching, i. 5–10.
   (b) The preaching of the gospel at Thessalonica, ii. 1–16.
      (i) The purity of the preachers' motives, ii. 1–6a.
      (ii) The preachers' refusal to accept maintenance, ii. 6b–9.
      (iii) The preachers' behaviour had been impeccable, ii. 10–12.
      (iv) The preachers' message the Word of God, ii. 13.
      (v) Persecution, ii. 14–16.

IV. THE RELATIONSHIP OF PAUL TO THE THESSALONIANS, ii. 17—iii. 13.
   (a) His desire to return, ii. 17, 18.
   (b) Paul's joy in the Thessalonians, ii. 19, 20.
   (c) Timothy's mission, iii. 1–5.
   (d) Timothy's report, iii. 6–8.
   (e) Paul's satisfaction, iii. 9, 10.
   (f) Paul's prayer, iii. 11–13.

V. EXHORTATION TO CHRISTIAN LIVING, iv. 1–12.
   (a) General, iv. 1, 2.
   (b) Sexual purity, iv. 3–8.
   (c) Brotherly love, iv. 9, 10.
   (d) Earning one's living, iv. 11, 12.

VI. PROBLEMS ASSOCIATED WITH THE PAROUSIA, iv. 13—v. 11.
   (a) Believers who died before the Parousia, iv. 13–18.
   (b) The time of the Parousia, v. 1–3.
   (c) Children of the day, v. 4–11.

VII. GENERAL EXHORTATIONS, V. 12–22.

VIII. CONCLUSION, v. 23–28.

I THESSALONIANS: COMMENTARY

I. GREETING (i. 1)

1. Letters in antiquity began with some variant of the formula 'A. to B. greeting', and this was usually followed by some pious expression, commonly a prayer. This was just as much part of the letter as our 'Dear Sir' at the beginning and 'Yours faithfully' or 'Yours sincerely' at the end (though the writer may be addressing his enemy, and be neither faithful nor sincere in what he writes). Here, for example, is a typical opening:

> 'Antonis Longus to Nilus his mother many greetings.
> And continually do I pray that thou art in health.
> I make intercession for thee day by day to the
> lord Serapis'.[1]

After this preamble the writer begins his message. Paul used this conventional way of beginning, varying it according to circumstances; but in his hands it took on a characteristically Christian shape.

In this letter he associates Timothy and Silvanus with himself, but there seems little doubt that the body of the letter came from Paul. It bears the marks of his style, and gives no appearance of being composite. Notice that he feels no need to assert his apostolate (contrast 1 Cor. i. 1; 2 Cor. i. 1; Gal. i. 1 etc.), which may point to the amicable relations between Paul and this church.

Though this is the shortest of the extant superscriptions it contains all the elements which appear in the fully developed form: the address to the church, the linking of the church with the Father and the Son, and the characteristic prayer for grace and peace. The address *unto the church of the Thessalonians* is unique, though not unlike that in Galatians, another early Epistle, and it may, as Milligan thinks, indicate that the local

[1] A. Deissmann, *Light from the Ancient East*, London, 1927, p. 188.

gathering of the believers is in mind, rather than the Church universal as in the later letters.

Also peculiar to these Epistles is the phrase *in God the Father*, Paul's habit being to say 'in Christ'. The mention of the two Persons together is a striking, if incidental, indication of the oneness of the Father and the Son. Being *in* the Father and the Son is a way of expressing the closeness of the relationship linking the Thessalonian believers with their God.

Paul's greeting is *Grace be unto you, and peace* (the words which follow in AV are absent from the oldest MSS). This looks like a combination of the usual Greek and Hebrew forms of salutation, but with a slight, though significant, change in the Greek, namely from *chairein* ('greeting') to *charis* ('grace'). This is one of the great Christian words. Cognate with *chara* ('joy'), it means basically 'that which causes joy'. In a Christian context that refers above all to the act of God in Christ whereby man's sin is put away and salvation made available as a free gift. From this it comes to mean any free gift of God, and in greetings it is used in this general sense, though with a glance at God's great gift to men.

With us *peace* is a negative concept, denoting the absence of war. But the Hebrew equivalent, *shalom*, is concerned with 'wholeness', 'soundness', and signifies prosperity in the widest sense, especially prosperity in spiritual things. When the Old Testament was translated into Greek, *shalom* was rendered by *eirēnē* (which we have here), and thus, for those steeped in the Old Testament, *peace* is this broad concept of the prosperity of the whole man, more especially including a flourishing state of soul.

There may be significance in the invariable order in which these words occur. First *grace*, then *peace*. There can be no true peace until the grace of God has dealt with sin.

II. PRAYER OF THANKSGIVING (i. 2-4)

2. Paul's prayer of thanksgiving is not simply a conventional opening, but a genuine expression of his feelings toward his converts. His prayer is constant, and he speaks of giving thanks for them all, so there were apparently no disaffected members. Like the Philippians, the Thessalonians seem to have been a continual joy to Paul.

3. The particular matters for which he gives thanks are listed, and we see an interesting conjunction of faith, hope, and love, as also in 1 Thes. v. 8, Rom. v. 2–5, Gal. v. 5f., Col. i. 4f., Heb. vi. 10–12, 1 Pet. i. 21f., and especially 1 Cor. xiii. 13. These widespread references seem to show that it was an accepted Christian practice to link these three graces, and not something that we necessarily owe to Paul.

The first point is *your work of faith*. In some of his writings, notably Romans and Galatians, Paul sets faith and works in sharp contrast. But the reason for this is to emphasize that salvation comes from faith and not at all from works, for 'by the deeds of the law there shall no flesh be justified in his sight' (Rom. iii. 20). But while he insists that salvation is all of God, he also insists that true faith is busy. For example, in Gal. v. 6, he speaks of 'faith which worketh by love'. So here he refers also to an activity which follows from the faith of the Thessalonians.

When he speaks of their *labour of love* Paul is not thinking of some deed of kindness done without hope of reward, as we usually do when we use this expression. The word *kopos* denotes laborious toil, and directs our minds to unceasing hardship borne for love's sake.

Love is our translation of the Greek *agapē*, a word not used very much before the Christians took it up and made it their characteristic word for love. Nygren, in his book *Agape and Eros* (London, 1953), has shown that the Christians not only made use of a new term, but that they had a new idea. *Eros*, basically signifying love between the sexes, may denote a very pure and lofty form of love. Essentially, however, it is a love of the worthy (or that which men think to be worthy) coupled with the desire to possess. Thus a man may set his affection on the moral ideal and desire to make it his own day by day, and this is no ignoble thing. But the Christian idea of love is something different, and finds its classic expression in Rom. v. 8, 'God commendeth his love toward us, in that, while we were yet sinners, Christ died for us'. This is the love of the completely unworthy. God loves, not because men are worthy, but because He is that kind of God, because it is His nature to love, because He *is* love. I think it is Emil Brunner who says that, if we speak about radium and omit to say that it is the radiant element, continually radiating itself away, we pass over that which really matters. So, if we speak of God's greatness, His righteousness and the like, but omit to say that He is love, we omit that which matters most of all. The really important thing is that God is love. By this we do not mean a theoretical love, but a love which is seen in the cross, a love which is always giving, a love which holds nothing back.

When this love comes to a man he is faced with a challenge he cannot ignore. Once he comes to see that God is like that, that God loves as part of His very nature, that God loves in a way which means Calvary, he must make a decision. Either he yields to the divine *agapē* to be transformed by it, to be re-made in the divine image, to see men in a measure as God sees them, or he does not. And if he does not, in that lies his condemnation. He has shut himself up to lovelessness. But those who yield themselves to God are transformed by the power of the divine *agapē*, so that they are content to give themselves in the service of others. Paul thanks God that this is what the Thessalonians have done.

The third cause for thanksgiving is their *patience of hope*, and again this must be understood carefully. *Hupomonē*, rendered *patience*, means not a negative, passive acquiescence, but an active, manly endurance: as Findlay puts it, 'not the resignation of the passive sufferer, so much as the fortitude of the stout-hearted soldier' (C.B.S.C.)[1] Hope, in a Christian context, always has an air of certainty about it. It is a confident expectation, and not the unfounded optimism which we often mean by the word. More particularly, the Christian hope is directed towards the second advent, which is possibly

[1]See also on 2 Thes. iii 5.

in mind here, especially if the phrase *in our Lord Jesus Christ* is connected with *hope* (as Findlay and Milligan think). Alternatively, it is grammatically possible to take these words as relating to all the preceding part of the verse, in which case they refer to the whole of the Christian life, which is then said to be lived in Christ (so Neil).

The addition *in the sight of God and our Father* draws attention to Fatherhood as the essence of the Christian view of God. It also links the Father and the Son in the most intimate way.

4. In these two Epistles Paul uses *brethren* twenty-one times, revealing the closeness of the tie which bound the proud Pharisee to the despised Gentile. Barriers insurmountable to men were done away in Christ. *Of God* should be connected with *beloved* (as RV), rather than with *election* (as AV). In the Greek *beloved* is a perfect participle, combining the thought of a love existing in the past with that of one continuing into the present with unabated force. This construction occurs only here in the New Testament (though Jude 1 is similar), and is richer in meaning than the usual expression (found for example in Rom. i. 7). In view of the many loose modern ideas on 'the brotherhood of man' it is worth noting that the New Testament concept of brotherhood is specifically a brotherhood in Christian bonds. Here it is linked with being loved by God and with election. Both are significant.

Paul speaks of knowing their *election*. In both Testaments we have the thought that God has chosen out His people. In the Old Testament this choice is usually associated with the nation, and in the New with individuals. The thought that God has chosen us to be His is another way of reminding us that our salvation is all of God, and not at all owing to our own efforts. In the face of those who think of election as harsh and arbitrary the teaching of this verse should be stressed, namely that election proceeds from God's love for us. It is usually held that one man cannot know that another is elect, but Paul here says that he knows the election of the Thessalonians. His reasons for this appear to be given in verse 5.

III. REMINISCENCES (i. 5—ii. 16)

a. Response of the Thessalonians to the original preaching (i. 5-10)

5. In his thought Paul now goes back to the original preaching at Thessalonica. He speaks of *our gospel*, the term emphasizing the message rather than the act of preaching, and reminding us that Christianity is essentially good news of action taken by God to bring salvation to sinful men. The possessive *our* may indicate that apostles, just as much as other men, need the gospel message, or, more probably, that the gospel was not something they knew in theory only, but something they had made their own. When Paul says that the gospel *came* to them he may be implying that it possesses a vital force; it is not simply so many words. True, the gospel must be proclaimed in words; but Paul insists that eloquence is not a complete explanation of its effectiveness; it came also *in power*. See Rom. i. 16, and cf. Nygren's comment: 'The gospel is not the presentation of an idea, but the operation of a power. When the gospel is preached . . . the power of God is at work for the salvation of men, snatching them from the powers of destruction . . . and transferring them into the new age of life.'[1] His next point is that the gospel was *in much assurance*, which in the Greek is closely linked with the Holy Spirit (there is no repetition of the *en*), and directs us to the inward assurance that the power of the Spirit had given both to the apostles and to their converts.

6. At the end of the last verse Paul had appealed to the manner of life of his companions and himself while in Thessalonica, as an illustration of the gospel. Now he indicates that the converts had heeded this example. They had become 'imitators' (not simply *followers* as AV) of the preachers and of their Lord. Notice here the conjunction of *much affliction* with *joy of the Holy Ghost*. Affliction has always been part of the lot of the true disciple of Christ, as He Himself foretold (Jn. xvi. 33). Luther asked, 'If Christ wore a crown of thorns, why

[1] *Commentary on Romans*, London, 1952, p. 67.

should His followers expect only a crown of roses?'[1] But just
as it is true that the Christian will find trouble in the world, so
it is true that he will have a joy which the world can never
take away (Jn. xvi. 22), a joy brought by the Holy Spirit to
the heart of the believer (Gal. v. 22).

7, 8. Paul has appealed to the example set by the apostles
(verse 5). Now he points out that the converts in their turn had
become examples to others. The word *tupos*, translated
ensamples, meant originally the mark of a stroke or blow (the
'print' of Jn. xx. 25), then a figure formed by a blow, an impression left by a seal or die, an image generally (Acts vii. 43),
and so it came to mean a pattern (IITh. viii. 9), which is its
meaning here. This is high praise, for in the first place Paul
calls no other church a pattern, and in the second he thinks of
them as examples, not only to the heathen, but to Christians
throughout Greece. Indeed, the reputation of his Thessalonian converts was world-wide. The word rendered
sounded out (*exēcheō*) is picturesque and might describe the
clarion call of a trumpet, or the roll of thunder. It certainly
emphasizes the resounding nature of the witness borne by the
Thessalonian church. The verb is a Greek perfect, which
implies that the sounding out was continuing. It was no
passing whim.

The word of the Lord is a phrase very familiar from the
prophetic writings of the Old Testament, and found often in
Acts, but only here and in 2 Thes. iii. 1 in the Pauline writings
(though it is not very different from expressions like 'the word',
'the word of God', 'the gospel of God' and the like, which are
frequent in Paul). It emphasizes the conviction of the Early
Church that the word they proclaimed was not the product of
human wisdom, but truly of divine origin. This word is said to
have sounded out *in Macedonia and Achaia*, the two provinces
which together embraced all Greece, and also *in every place*. This
may be a hyperbole, but there may be a glance at the fact that
Aquila and Priscilla had come to Corinth from Rome just

[1]Cited in Neil.

before Paul wrote this letter (Acts xviii. 2), and what was known at Rome could be presumed to be known everywhere.

The sentence looks as though it ought to end at *place*. But it is typical of Paul's impetuous style that he should go off on a new tack where a more conventional writer would finish. So he says that the faith of the Thessalonians is so universally spoken of that he himself has no need to say anything about it.

9, 10. *They themselves* is sometimes taken to indicate people from Macedonia and Achaia, but is probably quite general. Anyone at all might be found telling of what was going on in Thessalonica (cf. Moffatt, 'people tell us of their own accord about the visit we paid to you'). It is not usual in such a context to speak of an *entering in*,[1] but the term is not difficult to understand. The indirect interrogative *what manner of* reminds us of the success of the visit, a success evident from the following statements.

Paul goes on to describe the conversion of the Thessalonians, and since much of the characteristic Pauline terminology is lacking from his description (e.g. justification by faith), it would seem that he is using the accepted mission terminology. It is reasonably clear that the first Christian preachers had a common understanding of the essence of their message, and that they had a recognized vocabulary to describe it and its effects. Paul seizes on three points.

First, they had turned away from idols, which must have been a very important part of the evidence of their conversion. In every age such action is a mark of the true Christian.

Secondly, they had come to *serve the living and true God*. A negative attitude is not sufficient. The word rendered *serve* really means 'serve as a slave' and reminds us of the way in which Paul delighted to call himself a 'slave of Jesus Christ'. It underlines the wholehearted nature of Christian service. Notice that God is spoken of as *living*, which contrasts with dead idols, and *true*, which means 'genuine' over against the

[1] Deissmann, however, cites an example in a Latin letter of the second century A.D. (*op. cit.*, pp. 197–9).

shadowy and unreal. The conjunction of these two terms gives emphatic expression to Paul's essential monotheism.

Thirdly, they awaited the second advent. Today this doctrine is neglected in many quarters to our great loss, and its rediscovery is sorely needed; for as J. E. Fison says: 'It is precisely that kind of conversion which the church as well as the world needs today, and which only the rediscovery of a living eschatological hope can produce.'[1]

T. F. Glasson maintains that this is one of the first references to the second advent. He contends that it was not found in the teaching of Jesus, and indeed, does not appear until the Thessalonian correspondence. He thinks it originated in the Early Church's study of the Old Testament, and that a note of imminence and urgency was given by Caligula's attempt to place an image of himself in the Temple. This was interpreted as showing himself to represent anti-Christ and the herald of the End.[2] But this reconstruction is not in accordance with much in the Gospels, with early logia like Acts i. 11, iii. 20f., x. 42, with the implications of the Aramaic *maranatha* ('Our Lord, come!') of 1 Cor. xvi. 22, or with the way in which eschatology is integral to the whole gospel. The consummation is implied in the facts that the old has passed away, that in the coming of the Messiah the new age has dawned, and that the power of God is at work. 'This act of God must reach its climax in judgement, in the vindication of the just, and in the supreme, and final, and visible victory of the Lord' (Neil).

At the same time we must query Neil's further idea that the eschatological event is not an event in time at all. 'The Lord is always at hand and comes to every generation, and we pass the Judgment of Doomsday upon ourselves every living moment', he says. But while there is a valuable truth here, this is not what the New Testament means when it speaks of the second advent, nor in particular what Paul means in this verse. Throughout the New Testament it is clear that the advent referred to is an event which will bring this world as

[1] *The Christian Hope*, London, 1954, p. 80.
[2] See *The Second Advent*, London, 1947.

we know it to a decisive close. It is the consummation of the age, and it is difficult to see how we can do without the idea of this consummation.

At the end of verse 10 Paul speaks of *the wrath to come*, which is apparently connected with the End. C. H. Dodd and others have made a determined attempt to eliminate the idea of 'the wrath of God' by insisting that the New Testament gives us a picture of the wrath as an impersonal process of retribution following upon sin. But it is difficult to substantiate this. It is true that there are some passages, as here, where the wrath is not explicitly linked with God. But can it be seriously argued that Paul was thinking here of a wrath separate from God? The wrath is explicitly linked with God in a number of passages (see, e.g., Jn. iii. 36; Rom. i. 18, ix. 22; Eph. v. 6; Col. iii. 6; Rev. xi. 18, xiv. 10, 19, xix. 15), and the idea is often present in places where the wrath is not explicitly mentioned, such as 2 Thes. i. 7-9. In any case the New Testament writers always regard the universe as God's universe. If retribution follows upon sin, then it seems impossible to maintain that this takes place independently of God. And if this should be maintained, then we would be building up a picture of a God who is personally indifferent to sin. The concept of the wrath of God is a healthy corrective to such unmoral views of the Deity, and it stands for ever as a striking reminder that God's holy nature is totally opposed to every form of evil.

Heaven is plural in the Greek, and some have seen in it the Rabbinic idea of a plurality of heavens (cf. 2 Cor. xii. 2). But singular and plural are interchanged so much in the New Testament that it seems unwise to set much store by the occurrence of the plural here. *He raised* reminds us that the Scripture habitually refers the resurrection to the direct action of the Father. It is the mark of His vindication and approval of the atoning work of the Son. Notice the centrality of the resurrection, for even when Paul is thinking of the second advent he refers to Christ as the One *whom he raised from the dead.*

Delivered, rhuomenon, is really in the present, being as Frame says, a 'timeless participle'. The word means something like 'rescue', rather than 'redeem' (which is more specific, and signifies 'deliver by the payment of a price'), and puts the emphasis on the greatness of the peril, and the power of Him who delivers. The completeness of the deliverance is underlined by the use of the preposition *ek*: we are delivered right 'out of' the wrath.

(b) The preaching of the gospel at Thessalonica (ii. 1–16)

We come now to a more direct defence of the apostle's conduct, with the Jewish slanders much in mind.

(i) The purity of the preachers' motives (ii. 1 6a). Verse 1

links up with i. 9, the unusual word *eisodos* being repeated (there it is translated *entering in*, here *entrance*), while *for yourselves* corresponds to *they themselves*. What other people reported of the Thessalonian church they themselves knew to be true. This opening has a twofold object: it shows Paul's confidence in the Thessalonians, and it directs their attention to a well-known fact which will refute the accusations of his opponents. If the result of his preaching was so manifest and so definite, then clearly he could not have been the time-server he was now accused of being.

In a masterly understatement Paul goes on to say that his entrance *was not in vain* ('our visit to you was no failure', Moffatt, Phillips), the Greek perfect tense giving the idea of a continuing result. It was not only that there was an impressive result at the time of the preaching, but a permanent change was wrought in the lives of the believers. The word *kenos*, rendered *in vain*, carries the idea of emptiness, and is a strong repudiation of any thought that Paul had frittered his time away in aimless pursuits. He had come with a definite aim, and he had secured what he had aimed at.

2. Greek has more than one word for 'but'; *alla*, the one used here, is a strong adversative, putting the following words in emphatic contrast with the preceding. Far from his visit being in vain, Paul and his companions were bold in their preaching of the gospel. He reminds his readers of the circumstances under which his little band first came to the city, drawing attention both to their physical suffering (*we had suffered before*), and to their mental trials (*were shamefully entreated*). At Philippi the preachers had undergone the painful punishments of scourging and having their feet fastened in the stocks. Neil thinks that the Pauline correspondence as a whole, and 2 Cor. xi. 23ff. in particular, indicate that Paul may have been specifically sensitive to bodily pain, so that he recalled it with something akin to horror. If this is so then his fortitude in the face of continual ill-treatment is something to marvel at, and indicates courage of the very highest order.

But his choice of words here directs attention not only to physical pain, but to the indignities which had been heaped on the Roman citizen at Philippi. *Shamefully entreated* (*hubristhentes*) indicates an attitude of haughty insolence on the part of the oppressors.

Despite these troubles the apostolic band had preached boldly. The verb rendered *we were bold* is derived from two Greek words, *pas rhēsis*, meaning 'all speech', so that basically it denotes a complete freedom of speech, and hence the feeling of being completely at home. This includes being without fear, and having complete confidence. It is difficult to find one English word which will express both these ideas, and usually our translations choose one and leave the other (though here Moffat says 'we took courage and confidence in our God'). In the New Testament the verb is always connected with the preaching of the gospel. Notice that here it is connected with *in our God* (an expression, incidentally, which is very characteristic of these two Epistles), for Paul is not speaking of merely natural courage, but of the supernatural endowment with which God equips those who put their trust in Him.

In this confidence and courage they had proclaimed the gospel, which is here characterized as *the gospel of God*. In i. 5 it is *our gospel*, for the preachers were proclaiming not something theoretical, but something which they knew for themselves and had made their very own. Here the aspect which is singled out for attention is that the gospel is not of human origin. It is nothing less than God's plan for man's salvation. Our age can do with the reminder that the Christian faith is not the accumulated wisdom of pious souls, nor the insight of men of religious genius, but the divine plan for dealing with man's sin.

But at Thessalonica, as at Philippi, there had been opposition, and this is brought out in the expression *with much contention*. Frame thinks this may indicate inward trouble. In this context, however, this is unlikely, since Paul is here occupied with those things which might have made him fear.

3. He finds it necessary, apparently, to insist on the purity of the motives of the preachers. From this it would seem that he is meeting an accusation that, like the many itinerant preachers of strange cults and philosophies, their interest was not in their message, but in their profits. *Our exhortation* is the manner of the preaching, as *the gospel of God* in the previous verse was the matter.

Paul makes three points. The preaching was *not of deceit* (though the word *planē* means 'error' rather than 'deceit'), *nor of uncleanness* (which points to an accusation of immorality. Religious prostitution was characteristic of many of the cults of the day, and it is clear that Paul was being accused of gross sensuality), *nor in guile* (pointing us to cunning craft: it properly signified catching fish with a bait, and thence came to mean any crafty design for deceiving or catching). There is an interesting change from *of* with the first two words to *in* with the last. The Greek *ek* denotes origin; but *en* rather signifies atmosphere, so that Paul is saying that his preaching did not spring from delusion or impurity, nor was it conducted in an atmosphere of craft.

4. The apostle vigorously repudiates these slanders, emphasizing the solemnity of his commission. So far from his seeking anything for himself, he could speak only because he was *allowed of God to be put in trust with the gospel*. His own subservient position is brought out in this expression, and so is the transcendent nature of his message. It was of divine origin, and therefore the accusation that he spoke from error was false. The verb *dokimazō*, rendered *allowed*, really means 'proved', 'tested', and so 'approved'. Our translation misses the force of the perfect tense in the Greek, the idea being 'we have been approved'. Paul thinks of himself as having been tried out by God, and then trusted for service. And it is out of this situation that he and his companions can speak, the present tense in *even so we speak* showing this to be their habitual practice.

He is emphatic that the message originated with God, and that it was not aimed at pleasing men. The word *pleasing* probably means more than the simple English term suggests. In the Greek there is the idea of service in the interests of others (see Moulton-Milligan for examples of this use from the inscriptions). The point is that, while Paul served men, he did not live to serve them. His service was primarily service of God, and he delighted to refer to himself as 'the slave of God', or 'of Christ'. This is something which still needs emphasis, for the Christian preacher is always tempted to accommodate his message to the desires of his hearers. Men do not want a message which tells them that they are nothing more than helpless sinners in God's sight, and must depend humbly on God's mercy for their salvation. They are more interested in the 'social implications' of the gospel. These, of course, must not be soft-pedalled. But the preacher must always put his emphasis on those doctrines to which Scripture itself gives priority.

That the Godward emphasis in Paul's preaching demands complete sincerity on the part of the preacher is brought out by the following *which trieth our hearts*. *Trieth* is the same verb as that rendered *allowed* in the earlier part of the verse, and signifies 'put to the test', passing over to 'approved by test'. *Heart* should not be interpreted as meaning only the emotions. In the Bible it denotes rather the sum total of our inward dispositions, including the intellect and the will as well. The whole of the motives and thoughts of the preacher are always open to God, and Paul maintains that his preaching was in the full consciousness of this fact. It is not unlike calling God to witness his sincerity, as he does in the next verse.

5, 6a. Having put positively the truth that his preaching was always done as in the sight of God, Paul now turns from the general to the particular, and from the positive to the negative, giving three things from which the preaching at Thessalonica had been free.

The first is flattery. Paul's words mean literally 'neither have we come to be in a word of flattery'. The verb conveys the idea of entering into and continuing in a given condition (as in Rom. xvi. 7 of Andronicus and Junia coming to be and continuing to be in Christ). 'In a word' refers to the totality of the preaching, but the remaining word *kolakias* is difficult to convey exactly in English. It is not flattery in the sense of fair, but insincere, words. Rather it denotes something like 'cajolery', the use of acceptable speech with the purpose of lulling another into a sense of security, so that one may obtain one's own ends. Paul emphatically repels the idea.

The second thing which he disclaims is *a cloke of covetousness*. The *cloke* is the giving of a reason which is plausible in itself, but which is not the real reason. It is only a pretext. *Covetousness* is more than the desire for money, and denotes the attitude of eager seeking to have more. While it is often shown in the desire for money, it is the spirit of desire in its most general sense, self-aggrandisement. Solemnly calling God to witness Paul disavows any such motive. He had not sought anything for himself when he evangelized the Thessalonians.

Paul's third disclaimer is of any seeking of glory from men, whether the Thessalonians or any others. This is a repetition of what he has already said in verse 4, with this difference, that before he was denying that he directed his preaching to serve the ends that men approved, whereas now he is thinking of his own inner state. He was not looking for the satisfaction that comes when one's work is praised. Paul did obtain honour, and to this day is honoured by countless thousands throughout the world. But he says that he did not *seek* honour, and it is this purity of motive which makes him a worthy object of the praise which Christians have always delighted to lavish upon him.

(ii) The preachers' refusal to accept maintenance (ii. 6b–9.)

The end of verse 6 forms a transition from the previous thought to that which is to follow, the connecting link being the expression translated *burdensome (en barei)*. The noun can signify either 'burden' or 'importance'. If it has the latter sense here, the meaning is that the apostles might well have been accounted worthy of honour, though they had not sought it, as the earlier part of the verse makes clear. If the former is the sense, the reference is to their right to maintenance, a subject to which Paul now turns his attention. The expression rendered *might have been* makes it quite clear that Paul thinks he and his companions had the full right to what follows. Only they did not exercise that right.

He refers to himself and his companions as *apostles of Christ*. *Apostle* means 'one who is sent', 'a messenger', and the term was in common use both among Jews and pagans. The Jews used the term to denote a man's personal representative, and the Talmud says more than once 'A man's *shaliach* is as it were himself' (*shaliach* being the Hebrew equivalent of the Greek *apostolos*, 'apostle'). Dom Gregory Dix and others reason from this that the apostles had the full authority of Christ, and that in due course they transmitted this authority to the bishops. This becomes the basis of a theory which sees the essential ministry of the Church in a divinely ordained episcopate charged with full apostolic authority. However T. W. Manson has shown[1] that too much has been claimed for the *shaliach*. In particular he makes it clear that the authority of the *shaliach* was limited to the terms of his original commission and that it was quite untransferable.

We see the essence of apostleship in the original commission given in Mk. iii. 14: 'he ordained twelve, that they should be

[1] In his book *The Church's Ministry*, London, 1948.

with him, and that he might send them forth to preach.' The essential task falling to the lot of the apostle was the proclamation of the gospel. Doubtless there were other things, such as the organization of, and provision for, a ministry for new churches, and the exercise of oversight; but these things were secondary. Paul could regard the proclamation of the authentic gospel as so much a part of the work of the apostle that he could say 'though we, or an angel from heaven, preach any other gospel unto you than that which we have preached unto you, let him be accursed' (Gal. i. 8). Apostleship is not something which conferred an honour upon a man, so much as something which laid an obligation upon him.

The apostles here are said to be *of Christ*. Apostleship is always conferred by a divine call, and not by human commissioning. Thus in Acts i the prayer before lots were cast on Joseph and Matthias ran 'shew whether of these two thou hast chosen'. The apostle was already chosen, and the only thing remaining was for him to be made known. So, when it was revealed that Matthias was the man, we read of no commissioning; simply that 'he was numbered with the eleven apostles'.

Thus, when Paul recalls here the fact that the preachers were apostles he is remembering the divine call which had set them apart to preach the gospel. It did give them a place of honour and authority, but he insists that they had not claimed such a place, and indeed goes on to show that they had been more conscious of their responsibility than of their privileges.

7-9. When the preachers had been among the Thessalonians, far from trying to make any gain of them, they had done all that they could for them. Paul speaks tenderly of their relationship, but the exact meaning of his words in verse 7 is not easy to discern. AV reads *we were gentle*, but a variant runs 'we were (or became) babes'. There is a difference of one letter only in the Greek (*ēpioi* 'gentle' and *nēpioi* 'babes'), and as this letter is the last letter of the preceding word it is easy to conjecture either that it was slipped in accidentally from that

word, or that it was omitted by a scribe who had already
written one *n*. The difficulty is made the more acute by the
fact that, while 'gentle' seems to give the better sense, 'babes'
has the better manuscript attestation. In favour of 'gentle' are
these considerations: it is hard to think of Paul comparing
himself to a babe and a nurse in the same sentence; *nēpios* has
the thought of being undeveloped and unripe, and when Paul
uses it, it generally has some note of blame; *ēpios* occurs in the
New Testament elsewhere only at 2 Tim. ii. 24, and there is
always a tendency for less usual forms to be assimilated to the
more usual. In favour of *nēpioi* is the manuscript evidence;
the fact that Paul has no great objection to mixing his metaphors, and in fact likens himself both to a father (verse 11) and
an orphan (verse 17 where *being taken* is literally 'being
orphaned') in this very chapter; after *apostles* in the previous
verse a noun is more likely than an adjective; the Greek
expression rendered *among you* is natural after 'babes', less so
after 'gentle'; and what Westcott and Hort call 'the change
from the bold image to the tame and facile adjective' which
they think 'characteristic of the difference between St. Paul
and the Syrian revisers'.[1]

With the evidence so evenly balanced a firm decision is not
possible, but I am inclined to accept the preponderance of
manuscripts and think of 'babes' as original. While it would be
easy to alter the original either way, the probability of an
alteration from 'babes' to 'gentle' is much greater than the
reverse. If this be the reading then the meaning would seem to
be (with Origen and Augustine) 'like a nurse among her
children talking in baby language', and so would indicate the
tender way the preachers adapted themselves to their hearers.
They took up no attitude of superiority.

The word *cherisheth* is the translation of *thalpē*, the Greek
verb meaning basically 'to warm'. It is used of the mother
bird (Dt. xxii. 6), and so comes to have the secondary meaning
'to cherish', 'to care for tenderly'. The probable meaning of

---

[1]'Notes on Select Readings', p. 128 (Appendix to *The New Testament in the
Original Greek*, Introduction, London, 1907).

her (heautēs) children is that the nurse is also the mother, and thus would give them very special care.

Paul's contention is that the apostles behaved in a genuinely affectionate manner towards the Thessalonians, and this he reiterates in different language in verse 8. Here *being affectionately desirous (homeiromenoi)* is the participle of an unusual verb, and, while it cannot be proved, Wohlenberg's conjecture that it may be a term of endearment derived from the nursery[1] is very attractive, and may well be right. At any rate the verb does express a yearning over the Thessalonians, and a good will which is repeated in *we were willing* ('we were well pleased', *ēudokoumen*).

The preachers were well pleased to impart, not only the gospel, *but also our own souls*. The Greek term *psuchē* does not mean quite what 'soul' does with us, but in such a context as this stands for the whole personality, 'our own selves' (RSV). The thought is of that giving of oneself (and not simply a message which one has heard somewhere) which is of the very essence of all genuine Christian teaching and evangelistic activity. There is an intensity of expression here which we should note, for much of our service is of that tepid sort which keeps our innermost self to ourself. It may be that this is at the root of much modern ineffectiveness. It is still true that vital Christian service is costly.

Part of the reason for Paul's giving of himself is seen in the concluding words of the verse, which really mean 'for you became beloved to us', 'beloved' signifying the self-giving quality of *agapē* (see on i. 3).

Paul now calls on his readers to remember the physical toil that the preachers had endured. *Labour (kopos)* is laborious toil, with the notion of weariness in labour, while *travail (mochthos)* directs attention to the hardship undergone. The combination (which, as Neil, following Lightfoot, points out, employs similar sounds, like our 'toil and moil') stresses the reality and fatiguing character of the work done. Paul and his companions were not play-acting, but they had had to work

[1]Cited in Milligan.

hard to discharge their double function of keeping themselves
and evangelizing, and that the Thessalonians knew right well.
The type of work is not mentioned, but Acts xviii. 3 tells us
that Paul was a tentmaker, which probably means a worker in
leather.

The reason for this constant work (cf. *night and day*), Paul
says, was that *we would not be chargeable unto any of you* (the word
chargeable (*epibareō*) is from the same root as that rendered
burdensome in verse 6) as *we preached unto you the gospel of God*.
The word *preached* denotes the action of a herald in proclaiming
what was given him to say. The essence of the herald's
work was to pass on a message, not to produce some high-
flown oration elaborately adorned with ear-tickling
phraseology, nor even to give a simple message to meet the
need as he saw it. The fact that this is a favourite way of
referring to the activity of the Christian preacher in the New
Testament puts stress on the divine nature of the message.
The gospel preacher is not at liberty to substitute his view of
the need of the moment for the God-given message of the cross.
This is underlined in the present passage by the reference to
the gospel of God, an expression we have met in verses 2, 8, and
substantially in verse 4. This deep-seated certainty that he was
entrusted with a message of divine, not human, origin, gave
a note of urgency and conviction to all that Paul did and said.
It is a reminder to us of the function of the Christian preacher,
and of an important factor in fervent and effectual preaching,
whether in the apostolic age or any other.

**(iii) The preachers' behaviour had been impeccable
(ii. 10–12).** Paul solemnly maintains that the Thessalonians
can bear testimony on his behalf (the *ye* is emphatic), and does
not hesitate to say that God is witness also (cf. verse 5), so
certain is he that his conscience is clear on the matter. He uses
three adverbs to describe the conduct of the preachers, and the
older commentators sometimes divided them up, taking the
first to refer to their behaviour towards God, the second
towards the Thessalonians, and the third towards themselves.

But this division seems artificial for, as Trench says, the Scripture 'recognizes all righteousness as one, as growing out of a single root, and obedient to a single law'.[1] The first word, *holily*, is often used in the sense 'religiously', while the second, *justly*, basically signifies conformity to a norm, and that norm for Biblical writers is the law of God. The third, *unblameably*, means without cause for reproach. The combination makes an impressive witness to Paul's certainty that no fair accusation could be levelled at the conduct of the little band of evangelists, and the fact that he so confidently appeals to the Thessalonians as witnesses to all this shows it could not be refuted.

Notice the expression *you that believe*. Christians are often spoken of in the New Testament simply as 'believers', so central is faith to the Christian scheme of things. But here it is probably used not only of Christians as opposed to non-Christians, but with the Jewish opponents of the apostles in mind. Although there were those who violently rejected the message and the messengers, Paul has confidence in the believers.

11, 12. From the way the preachers had lived and commended the message Paul turns to the content of the message, and reminds (*as ye know*) his readers of the tenderness with which the gospel had been preached to them, and of the thoroughgoing nature of the demands that had been made upon them. He himself had been like a father to them, the very antithesis of the deceiver and go-getter he had been misrepresented as being. His loving care is brought out in his insistence that he had brought the message to *every one* (the Greek 'each one' being more emphatic than the simple 'each'). In other words he had not contented himself with giving the message in general terms to the Thessalonian public at large, but he had been sufficiently interested in individuals to bring it home to them one by one, evidently in private conversations (cf. Phillips, 'how we dealt with each one of you personally').

Paul uses three verbs to convey the manner of the preaching,

[1]*Synonyms of the New Testament*, London, 1880, p. 329.

the combination giving the impression of urgency. The apostles had evidently been very much in earnest. But with it there is also the note of tenderness, the second verb, *comforted*, showing that Paul had had regard to the difficulties under which they laboured. Outside this Epistle this verb occurs in the New Testament only in Jn. xi. 19, 31, where it is used of comforting the bereaved.

But though there is this definite note of tenderness and understanding, it is also clear that the message was uncompromising, for the demand was made *that ye would walk worthy of God*, which gives us, as Findlay says, 'the noblest possible ideal of life' (C.B.S.C.). Clearly Paul had not toned down the demands of the gospel in any way and we are reminded that, when we become followers of the Christ, no less a demand is made on us.

Our version runs *who hath called you*, but the better manuscripts read 'who calls you', the use of the present bringing home the fact that God's call is something that never ceases. On occasion Paul can use the aorist reminding us of the once-for-all nature of the call (e.g. Gal. i. 6, 15); and again he may make use of the perfect to draw attention to the fact that those called remain in the position of called ones (e.g. 1 Cor. vii. 15, 17). But here we see that God's call is always coming to us, and it calls us to nothing less than being worthy of Him. The Christian can never be content with a low standard.

God calls us *unto his kingdom and glory*, the two concepts here being closely linked (as we see from the Greek with its single preposition and article). The kingdom of God is the central topic of Jesus' teaching. It has Old Testament roots as well, for the idea that God rules over all is very ancient. But there was a new emphasis in the teaching of our Lord, and scholars today are increasingly agreed that for Him the concept was essentially dynamic; i.e. He thought of the kingdom as something that happens, as God's rule in action, rather than as a realm. In a sense the kingdom is present here and now, for there are those who have yielded themselves to God to do His will. In a sense it is future, for not yet do we see all His enemies put under His feet. It is closely associated with the Person of Jesus, and while the kingdom and the cross do not seem to be linked in so many words, we cannot but think that the death of the Christ was necessary to the establishment of the kingdom. It is a gift from God (Lk. xii. 32), and not the result of men's labours; it is not something that men can explain, but is always sheer miracle (Mk. iv. 26-29). The thought of the Gospels is that God has broken into this world of space and time, in the person of His Son, and so the kingdom is brought in.

The idea is not as central in the Pauline correspondence as in the Gospels, but Luke tells us that Paul could describe his ministry at Ephesus in the words *among whom I have gone preaching the kingdom of God* (Acts xx. 25; cf. xxviii. 31); and important references to it do occur in the Epistles, a notable feature of Paul's understanding of it being that he can speak of the kingdom as Christ's, just as it is God's (Eph. v. 5; Col. i. 13). In the passage before us Paul has this great conception in mind.

(iv) The preachers' message the Word of God (ii. 13).

The manner in which Paul introduces his thanksgiving (*kai hēmeis*) leads some to think that he is answering a letter which had been written to him from the Thessalonians, further evidence for this being the way stages in the argument are introduced in iv. 9, 13, v. 1, and the repeated *ye know* (which is taken as meaning 'as you said') in i. 5, ii. 1, 5, 11, iii. 3, 4. Rendel Harris argued the case in *The Expositor*,[1] and this point of view has been accepted by Frame, Lake and others. It is quite possible, but the evidence is far from conclusive, and it may be simply that Paul is answering points made by Timothy in a verbal report.

The matter of the thanksgiving is that they received the message which was preached to them as truly *the word of God*. Twice over Paul insists that this was what the Thessalonians had heard. The second time is particularly emphatic as we may see from Findlay's rendering, 'you accepted no word of

[1] Fifth Series, Vol. VIII, pp. 168ff.

men, but, as it truly is, God's word' (C.G.T.) Paul could preach with certainty and power, for he had the profound conviction that what he said was not of man's devising, but in very truth the word of God. The Christian Church cannot do without this conviction. To preach interesting little moral essays can never prove an adequate substitute for the word which comes from God.

There are two different words for *received* in this verse, and Neil is of opinion that the former, *paralambanō*, is a technical word for the reception of the *kērugma*, the message preached by the evangelists, citing its use in iv. 1, 1 Cor. xv. 3, xi. 23 in confirmation. Be that as it may, it denotes something rather formal and outward; whereas the other word, *dechomai*, conveys the idea of a welcome, being the usual word for the reception of a guest. So the word of God was not only heard and received by the Thessalonians; it was welcomed.

At the end of the verse Paul makes the point that this *word of God* is something which does things (as, in Rom. i. 16, the gospel is said to be 'the power of God.' Most accept the AV translation *which effectually worketh* (or something equivalent). But Armitage Robinson, in a valuable note on *energein* and its cognates in his commentary on Ephesians (pp. 241–7), argues that it should be understood as passive, i.e. 'is made operative', his point being that, while another writer might well have used the active, Paul prefers the passive which implies that God is the One who works. Whether we accept Robinson's linguistics or not, this is certainly the thought of Paul, for God is the effective power and the word His instrument. This verb, incidentally, is almost always used in the New Testament with reference to supernatural activity.

(v) Persecution (ii. 14–16). The evidence of this working of God in the converts was seen in their activity. They became 'imitators' (not *followers* as AV) of the Christian churches in Judæa, which are apparently singled out for mention because of the persecutions they had had to endure. We have no exact knowledge of the details of these persecutions (though from

Acts we can see the sort of thing that must have happened); but clearly they were well known throughout the Christian Church so that Paul had no need to go into details.

15, 16. He proceeds to make the point that the conduct of the Jews has been consistent, they have always been hostile to the purpose of God. When he says that they *killed the Lord Jesus* he manages, by an unusual word order, to emphasize both *Lord* and *Jesus*. The One whom they killed was the Lord, with all that that means in terms of heavenly glory; and He was Jesus, fully man, and their fellow-countryman. Nor did this attitude begin with Jesus, for they also killed *their own prophets;* nor did it finish there, for they *have persecuted us.* There is a consistent attitude of opposition to God's way and God's people, and so *they please not God,* which is to be understood in the sense 'they are not pleasing to God', or 'displease God' (RSV). In like manner they oppose the best interests of men.

The indictment of the Jews is continued in verse 16. They have opposed the preaching of the news of God's saving act among the Gentiles. Salvation is the comprehensive term, of which such concepts as redemption, reconciliation and the like represent different aspects. It is sometimes viewed as being a salvation from evils such as wrath (Rom. v. 9), or perdition (Phil. i. 28); sometimes it is a salvation with a view to blessings, such as the heavenly kingdom (2 Tim. iv. 18). Here, as often, the term is used absolutely, with both positive and negative aspects implied.

The effect of the Jewish attitude is given in the latter part of the verse. Grammatically *to fill up their sins alway* expresses the purpose of the Jews; but the sense of it is that God's purpose is worked out in this way; their continual hostility to His plan inevitably brings His wrath upon them. The idea behind the phrase is that they piled sin upon sin (Phillips translates 'I fear they are completing the full tale of their sins'); and the inevitable consequence of this continuance in sin is that the wrath will be vented upon them. *Is come* in the Greek is in the aorist tense. This tense often denotes past action, but here the wrath is surely eschatological, and therefore future. The aorist here stresses the completeness and certainty of the coming of the wrath. The expression rendered *to the uttermost* might also be understood as 'at last', 'finally', and some commentators prefer this. But probably in this case the AV is to be preferred.

The denunciation of his own nation in these verses is unparalleled in the rest of the Pauline writings and gives some indication of the depth of Paul's feelings on the matter. As Neil says, he speaks like an Old Testament prophet, and his vigorous words leave no doubt as to the extent to which his nation had departed from the divine way. The castigation is unqualified, and the final expression indicative of the eschatological wrath leaves no hope for the future. A nation (or a man) can reach a point in opposition to God where return is impossible.

IV. THE RELATIONSHIP OF PAUL TO THE THESSALONIANS (ii. 17–iii. 13)
(a) His desire to return (ii. 17, 18)

17. Paul strongly desired to return to the scene of his labours, a desire arising from his deep regard for his converts. The *we* is emphatic, as is the *even I Paul* of the next verse, and the latter particularly singles Paul out from his coadjutors, and stresses his personal desire to see the converts.

The expression *being taken from you* means literally 'having been orphaned', and though the verb is used with some degree of freedom, being applied to other things than literal orphaning, yet it is a strong word, fastening attention on Paul's sense of desolation. Already in this chapter Paul has compared himself to a mother (verse 7) and a father (verse 11): this is another example of his complete readiness to mix his metaphors if only he can make his point. The thought of being orphaned emphasizes his affection for those to whom he writes. So does the following *in presence, not in heart*, where Phillips brings out the meaning by rendering, 'though never for a moment separated in heart'.

This feeling of longing for them is further expressed by his choice of the term translated *endeavoured*. The verb *spoudazō* combines the ideas of speed and diligence, and conveys an impression of eagerness, of making a quick and serious effort. In conjunction with this Paul uses the comparative adverb *perissoterōs, the more abundantly*. But as the comparative in the New Testament has practically taken over the functions of the superlative the meaning is probably elative, i.e. 'very abundantly', or, 'most abundantly' (though Milligan thinks the comparison is genuine, and paraphrases, 'we were exceedingly desirous to see you again face to face, and all the more so because of the hindrances we encountered'). The apostle's exceeding eagerness to see his friends is further emphasized by the phrase *with great desire*. The word *epithumia* means a strong passion, so that it is often translated 'lust' or 'covetousness'. This is one of the few places in the New Testament where it is used in a good sense.

18. Here the expression *we would have come* continues this stress on Paul's eagerness, *would* being the rendering of *ēthelēsamen*. There is some doubt as to whether this verb or *boulomai* is the stronger in the New Testament; but clearly Paul is again using a word which conveys his strong desire to visit his friends. *Once and again* translates the Greek expression *kai hapax kai dis* (lit. 'and once and twice') the meaning of which is not quite certain. Minus the first 'and' it is found four times in the Greek Old Testament, and each time it denotes a plurality of occasions without exact specification, something like our 'more than once'. This appears to be the meaning here. With 'and' prefixed the force will be, 'I wanted to come to you, and that more than once.'

However, the apostles had been prevented from doing so, and Paul attributes this to the activity of Satan. Just what form Satan's intervention had taken he does not specify, but evidently the Thessalonians knew enough to recognize the allusion. There are objections to all the suggestions that modern scholars have put forward. Thus some speak of illness on the part of Paul, but it would be remarkable if this applied to Silas and Timothy as well. Others explain it as meaning that Satan inspired the politarchs to demand such surety as would keep Paul and his companions away. But the Thessalonians would know more about this than the apostle, and it would seem hardly worth mentioning. There is also the difficulty of the *once and again*. It seems best, therefore, to confess our ignorance of the circumstances, and to understand the term in the most general sense.

Paul has no doubt in his mind regarding the activity of the evil spirit he calls Satan. We read of him again as *the tempter* (iii. 5), and probably as 'the evil one' in 2 Thes. iii. 3 (see note there); while elsewhere Paul refers to 'the god of this world' (2 Cor. iv. 4), and 'the prince of the power of the air' (Eph. ii. 2). It is clear that Paul thought of Satan as having real existence, and Ramsay's idea that the term is used figuratively here and throughout the New Testament[1] is to be rejected.

(b) Paul's joy in the Thessalonians (ii. 19, 20)

19. This Epistle is, for the most part, very practical, but Paul at this point is almost lyrical in his expressions of esteem for his converts. He speaks of them as *our hope*, our *joy*, and our *crown of rejoicing*, all three expressions pointing to his intense pride in them, as does the *our glory and joy* of the next verse. It is clear enough that he cannot find words too strong for what he wants to say.

The *crown* of which he speaks (the *stephanos*) is the laurel wreath given to the victor at the games, or the festive garland, rather than the *diadēma*, the royal diadem (though the distinction must not be pressed too strongly, as *stephanos* is sometimes used of the royal crown). The word *kauchēsis*, translated *rejoicing*, is sometimes rendered 'boasting' or 'glorying', and gives the impression of joy outwardly expressed as well as inwardly felt.

Probably we should take *Are not even ye* as a parenthesis, so

[1] *St. Paul the Traveller and the Roman Citizen*, London, 1930, p. 231.

that the meaning will be 'What is our hope . . . (Are not you?) in the presence, etc.' Notice how the title giving Him the highest place is combined with His human name in the phrase *our Lord Jesus* (*Christ* is not in the older MSS). This expression is more frequently used in the Thessalonian Epistles than anywhere else in the New Testament. In these eight chapters it is found twenty-four times, while in the much longer books, Acts and Romans, it is found only seventeen and sixteen times respectively. This frequent use of 'Lord' may well be because in these two letters the second coming is so much in Paul's mind. This is certainly the case here, for he goes on to refer immediately to *his coming*. This is the first occurrence of the word *parousia* in Christian literature. It means basically 'presence' (as in 2 Cor. x. 10 etc.), but it came to be used as the technical expression for a royal visit. Deissmann cites many examples of this use from the papyri.[1] In the New Testament it becomes the accepted word for the second coming of the Lord, and this is a typical example of its use.

20. There is an emphasis on both *ye* and *are*. The Thessalonians (and no other) are (and not will be) Paul's cause for pride and joy. Of the two words which he uses, *glory* refers to their giving him cause for honouring them before other people, and *joy* to his own feelings of delight. Outwardly and inwardly the Thessalonian converts crowned his ministry.

(c) Timothy's mission (iii. 1–5)

1. The chapter division here is unfortunate. *Wherefore* links what follows with what has preceded. It is 'on account of the things just mentioned', i.e. in ii. 17–20, that Timothy's mission was undertaken.

To whom does *we* refer in this verse? The first person plural is a problem throughout the Epistle. On the one hand, Silas and Timothy are associated with Paul in the opening salutation; on the other the style seems just as Pauline as in the Epistles accepted as coming from the great apostle's hand, and

[1] *Light from the Ancient East,* London, 1927, pp. 368–73.

some of the things said seem to refer to Paul alone. The difficulty is especially great here, and various solutions have been suggested. Some commentators draw attention to verse 5 with its emphatic use of the singular; and infer that the plural here is significant, and must apply to all three. There is an immediate difficulty in that it is hard to think of Timothy as included in the sending of himself (verse 2). This leads to the suggestion that Paul and Silas are meant.

I cannot think that this is an attractive solution. A plural applying to all three authors is understandable, and so is an editorial plural which means Paul only. But a plural meaning two out of three is difficult. Moreover *alone* at the end of the verse is also plural (*monoi*), although it is quite clear that it refers to Paul only, and the natural assumption is that the verb also refers to him only. Accordingly it would seem that *we* is editorial, and that the decision was Paul's, although we need not think that it was taken without consultation with his helpers.

Paul speaks of his anxiety becoming intolerable (taking the most probable meaning of the verb he employs). *Stegō* basically means 'to cover', and so it may mean 'to hide by covering', 'to conceal', and some accept this meaning here. But it may also mean 'to ward off by covering', and so 'to bear up against', 'to endure', and this gives the better sense in this passage. It is also the meaning of the verb in 1 Cor. ix. 12 and xiii. 7, its only New Testament occurrences outside this chapter.

Kataleipō, the word used by Paul to describe his being left at Athens, is a strong term, and on occasion can be used of abandoning (as in Eph. v. 31 of a man leaving his parents when he marries), and is often used of dying (as in Mk. xii. 19 of the dead man leaving his wife). It expresses a sense of desolation which is reinforced by the emphatic *alone*. It was with a very real sense of privation that Paul had said goodbye to Timothy. Though he knew that his helper's departure was necessary, he had felt himself abandoned. He had had to face the cultured philosophers and idolators of Athens, and to face them—alone.

2. Something of Paul's regard for Timothy comes out in his unusually elaborate reference to him (he is generally simply 'our brother'). We see, too, something of his high regard and deep concern for his friends in Thessalonica in that he was ready to part with such a beloved friend and valued servant of God at such a time. A complicated textual problem makes it difficult to be certain of the exact words Paul used to praise his coadjutor. *Timotheus, our brother*, is certain; but after that some MSS read 'and minister of God', some 'and fellow-labourer of God', some 'and fellow-labourer', some 'minister and fellow-labourer of God', and some 'minister of God and our fellow-labourer'. It would seem that our choice must be between 'minister of God', and 'fellow-labourer of God', the other readings being apparently attempts to deal with the problem set by these two. The manuscript attestation is more in favour of 'minister' than 'fellow-labourer'. But a strong argument for the latter reading is that, despite its occurrence in 1 Cor. iii. 9, 'fellow-labourer with God' is a startling expression, and scribes would be much more likely to alter 'fellow-labourer' to 'minister' than *vice versa*. On the whole, it seems slightly more probable that 'minister' (*diakonos*) is original, but we cannot be sure. This word was used eventually as a technical term to describe one of the orders of the ministry. But before it came to have this particular meaning of 'deacon', it was used of the service of a table waiter, then of service in general, and so of the specifically Christian service of God and man. It is used in this broad sense here.

The purpose of sending Timothy was *to establish you, and to comfort you concerning your faith*. Swete (on Rev. iii. 2) thinks that the verb *establish* was one of the technical words in the Pastoralia of the Early Church, and it may well have been. In meaning the verb has the notion of strengthening (*stērizō*, from *stērinx*, a 'support'). It occurs often in the New Testament and brings home to us that it is not sufficient to have had a spectacular conversion. We must go on from there to be established and strengthened in the faith. *Parakaleō* means rather more than 'comfort' in our sense of the term; it, too, has the notion of strengthening, perhaps by way of exhortation or encouragement. Etymologically it denotes 'to call to the side of', and the noun from this root was used of the counsel for the defence in a law-suit, one who was called alongside to help (cf. 1 Jn. ii. 2 and the use of the term to denote the Holy Spirit, Jn. xiv. 16, 26, etc.). So we get the idea of strengthening, aiding, encouraging, exhorting. If we are to render the verb by 'comfort' it must be in its original sense in accordance with the Latin derivation (*con fortis*). It is not a gentle soothing, but a fitting for the battle. *Concerning* does not seem the most apt way of rendering the preposition *huper*, which here may retain some of its original force of 'for the advantage or benefit of', as Milligan thinks.

3. Paul's purpose in sending Timothy is further elaborated. There is some difficulty about the meaning of *sainesthai*, translated *be moved*. Something like AV is the usual view; but the verb is used by Homer and others of a dog wagging its tail, and so comes to signify 'to fawn upon', 'to flatter'. If we accept this as the sense here (and the meaning of the word indicates that we should), then Paul is saying that Timothy's mission was in order that the Thessalonians should not be cajoled with smooth talk when they were in the midst of persecution and difficulties. It is likely that, while the Gentiles were persecuting them, the Jews were urging them to abandon the Christian way and accept Judaism, which would immediately free them from their plight. He does not say *by*, but *in* these afflictions, which strengthens the view that it is smooth talk of the Jews in the midst of the opposition of the Gentiles that is meant, rather than the opposition itself.

The concluding part of verse 3 is a sobering reminder that affliction is not to be taken as something strange and unusual for the believer. *We are appointed thereunto* writes Paul, and links himself with the Thessalonians in this necessary suffering of difficulties. The verb he uses (*keimai*, practically the perfect passive of *tithēmi*) is a strong one, and is used, for example, of 'a city set on an hill' (Mt. v. 14), and of Paul being 'set for the defence of the gospel' (Phil. i. 17). There is a sense of immovability about it, of unchangeable divine appointment. Affliction, then, is no accident, but a very necessary part of the life of the Christian (cf. Jn. xvi. 33; Acts xiv. 22).

4. Paul's certainty of the place of tribulation was not a new discovery, but something that had already occupied a place in his first preaching to the Thessalonians. Probably we should regard the use of the imperfect tense in the verb *proelegomen* as significant and translate 'we repeatedly foretold', which harmonizes with his reiteration that the Thessalonians knew these things. There is another hint at the certainty and divine ordination of tribulation in the verb rendered *should (mellomen,* not the simple future, this verb gives a similar note of divine assurance in Rom. viii. 13, 18, etc.). But Paul had not only made a prediction; his words had been fulfilled, as the Thessalonians could testify.

5. In this verse Paul reiterates the thought of verse 1. There is, however, a greater emphasis on his personal feeling and activity, for he takes the unusual course in this letter of using the first person singular (in the emphatic *kagō*). Those who think of the *we* of verse 1 as including Paul's friends naturally understand the *I* as referring, in contrast, to his personal action. But, as we have already noted that the earlier verse is best taken as referring to Paul alone, this statement should be understood as repeating and giving greater emphasis to what he has already said once.

T. W. Manson understands *pistin* in this verse as 'faithfulness', rather than *faith*, but seemingly on inadequate grounds. The word can have this meaning, and in this verse it would not be inappropriate. Its more usual meaning however, is 'faith', and as it seems to have that meaning in verse 2, it is better to take it in the same way here. Paul sent to make inquiry about their faith, i.e. whether it had survived the time of testing.

There is an interesting change of construction in the latter part of the verse. The use of the indicative in *lest by some means the tempter have tempted you* gives the impression that the writer thinks this has probably happened; but the change to the subjunctive *and our labour be in vain* makes the second possibility a matter open to doubt. Whereas Paul thinks it probable that Satan has applied pressure to his converts, he does not think it likely that they will have given way. He uses *kopos* for *labour*, a word which stresses the thought of wearisome toil. His ministry at Thessalonica had been no perfunctory one.

The tempter is an obvious reference to Satan whose activity as far as men are concerned is that of tempting to wrong action. See note on ii. 18.

(d) Timothy's report (iii. 6–8)

6. *But now* introduces a new section, marking a break in the Greek. It indicates that the letter was being written not long after Timothy had made his report. Moffatt renders 'a moment ago', which is a trifle too strong, but directs our attention to the fact that the arrival of the messenger was very recent.

Timothy's news is described as *good tidings*, Paul making use of the verb usually associated with the preaching of the gospel (*euangelizomai*), a fact which indicates how remarkably Paul was affected by Timothy's news. Indeed this is the only place in the New Testament where the word is used of any good news other than that of the saving work of God in Christ. For him the report he received was indeed a gospel, reminding him of the faithfulness and the power of God. It put new heart into him, and enabled him to go about his work with vigour and certainty.

Faith and charity. The former term expresses their attitude of trust in God, and the latter their attitude of love (for this is what *agapē* means, rather than 'charity' in our sense). The Thessalonians had not been wanting in the right attitude either to God or to man. But the good news did not finish there. Not only were the converts orthodox in doctrine and impeccable in conduct; they also retained warm feelings towards their

3   65

father in God. Here the personal note is struck. 'Having remembrance' of someone is sometimes used in the sense of remembering them in prayer; but in this context the general sense, and also the adjective *good*, which here means much the same as 'pleasant' (cf. RSV 'kindly'), indicate that the phrase has another meaning. This is reinforced by *desiring greatly to see us*, the verb *epipotheō* marking an intensity of feeling as in nearly all the passages where it is found (e.g. 2 Cor. v. 2; Phil. i. 8, ii. 26). The yearning for a reunion was mutual, and again we see something of Paul's tender regard for his Thessalonian converts.

7. *Brethren*. This form of address brings out the affection he felt for them. *Comforted*. Better 'encouraged' or 'strengthened', the verb being *parakaleo*, as in verse 2 (q.v.). The preposition in the phrase *over you* is *epi*, conveying the idea that his converts were the basis of the strengthening he had experienced. The same preposition occurs again in the following phrase where it is translated *in*; but this time the meaning is slightly different, and more in accordance with the literal meaning 'over'. It gives a hint of rising above the difficulties. At the end of the verse another preposition, *dia*, rendered *by*, gives the means whereby the comfort was brought.

Affliction and distress. Both words give the idea of pressure from without, the former (*anankē*) basically meaning 'the choking, pressing care', and the latter (*thlipsis*) 'the crushing trouble' (Lightfoot). They combine to emphasize that Paul's situation was far from being a happy one when the comfort he speaks of reached him. (See *Introduction*, p. 14.)

8. This leads to the thought that it is life to him to know that his converts are standing fast. We should probably take *now* as meaning 'at the present time', i.e. the apostle is expressing his state at the time he wrote, rather than recalling what he had felt when Timothy arrived. Some, however, take it to be logical, not temporal, and translate 'this being so'. He uses the present tense in the verb *live*; it is a continuing life that he experiences. That is to say, he did not receive a passing burst of inspiration from the news from Thessalonica, but something which remained, and would remain with him. There is an emphasis on the word *ye* which may indicate that Paul attached special importance to the Thessalonians' endurance. In a sense they were a test case, and the successful propagation of the gospel in other places depended on their standing firm as a living testimony to the power of God. Certainly Paul is stressing that for him much depended on them. The verb he uses for standing (*stēkō*) is not the usual one, but a late form which seems to have something of the idea of firmness about it, as in our translation *stand fast*. The construction in the conditional clause is unusual; *ean* usually takes the subjunctive, but here has the indicative which gives a touch of definiteness. As Findlay says, it 'states the hypothesis more assertively' than does the regular construction, and the clause 'is a virtual appeal: "You must show that my misgiving was needless; you will go on to justify my confidence" ' (C.G.T.).

(e) Paul's satisfaction (iii. 9, 10)

This leads Paul into a section in which he gives expression to his great satisfaction at the turn of events in Thessalonica, first by a rhetorical question, and then by a prayer that he might be able to come and see them.

9. *What thanks* (or better, 'thanksgiving') *can we render to God again for you?* he asks. By human standards what had happened was a tribute to the work Paul had done, and was something in the nature of a personal triumph, as Neil points out. The church had been so well established that, though the believers were young in the faith and had been subjected to such stern tests, they had come through with flying colours, and their founder might well feel proud of his work. But Paul saw things differently, and realized that what had happened was due to the divine power working in the believers, and thus he seeks to render thanks for God's goodness in this matter. The word *render again* (*antapodidōmi*) in the Greek carries with it the notion of something that is due (as in 2 Thes. i. 6; Lk. xiv. 14 etc.). There is probably a similar recognition of what

67

God has done in his joying *before our God* where, as Milligan says, he deepens the joy by referring it to its true Author.

10. Paul's fervent longing to see the Thessalonians again comes out strongly. Praying *night and day* is emphatic enough in itself, but he joins to it a very strong adverb in *huperek-perissou*, a word which is found elsewhere in the New Testament only in 1 Thes. v. 13 and Eph. iii. 20. It is a double compound, giving a twofold addition to the original 'abundantly', and one gets the impression of a man struggling to find words to express a feeling too deep for words.

Of the two words commonly used for prayer he chooses *deomai*, the word which expresses a feeling of need, of lack (rather than *proseuchomai*, which stresses more a sense of devotion to God). Combined with the adverb mentioned above, it draws marked attention to Paul's sense of loss in his separation from his friends and, by inference, to his regard for them.

The content of his continual prayer is twofold. He prays for reunion with them, not simply with a view to social intercourse, but *that we . . . might perfect that which is lacking in your faith*. The verb *katartizō* basically means 'to render complete', and might be used of such an activity as mending nets (Mt. iv. 21); but more commonly its use in the New Testament is metaphorical. It is translated 'restore' in Gal. vi. 1, where the idea is of correction and not of punishment. Sometimes it conveys the thought of equipping (Heb. x. 5, 'prepared'; xi. 3, 'framed'), or, as here, of supplying what is missing for the full discharge of the functions for which a thing or a person is designed.

That which is lacking is our translation of the Greek *husterēma*, a noun derived from the verb 'to come behind', 'to be left behind'. In spite of his great enthusiasm for the spiritual achievement of his Thessalonian converts, Paul yet recognizes that they come short of what they should be. Even in such a passage as this, where he is giving full rein to his desire to see them, and his joy in their stand, he yet finds a prominent place for this pastoral work of building them up wherever their faith is defective. It is a mark of Paul's tact in dealing with the situation that he speaks first of the things wherein he can sincerely praise them, before indicating that there are other aspects to be taken into consideration. Calvin found in this verse an indication of the importance of Christian teaching: 'From this it is clear how much we must devote ourselves to teaching. For teachers were not ordained only that in one day or in one month they should bring men to the faith of Christ, but that they should bring to completion the faith that has just begun' (cited in Neil).

(f) Paul's prayer (iii. 11-13)

From a rhetorical question Paul now turns to an actual prayer. His petition is twofold, first that he might be brought to Thessalonica, and secondly that the Thessalonians might increase in love.

11. Some have seen in the opening *Now God himself* an emphatic contrast, either with human activity in the preceding *praying*, or with Satan understood (cf. ii. 18). But this seems unnecessary, and the Greek may well be explained as simply the introduction of a new section, together with what Lightfoot calls 'an outburst of the earnest conviction which was uppermost in the Apostle's mind of the utter worthlessness of all human efforts without the divine aid'.

Notice that *our Lord Jesus Christ* is linked with *God himself and our Father* in the closest fashion in the address of this prayer, and also that the verb (*kateuthunai*) is in the singular. There could hardly be a more impressive way of indicating the lordship of Christ, and His oneness with the Father. In view of the early date of this letter this is evidence that from a very early time Christians accepted the deity of our Lord without question. (Prayer is no place for the introduction of argument.) Prayer is offered only to God; also, only One who was divine could be bracketed in this way with the Father. Cf. 2 Thes. ii. 16f. for a similar construction.

The verb *direct* is that rendered 'guide' in Lk. i. 79, and means 'to make straight'. In this context Paul is obviously seeking the removal from the way of the obstacles that Satan has put there.

12. The second part of his petition is introduced with an emphatic 'But you' (*humas de*). Whatever the Lord may have in store for Paul and his companions, he prays that spiritual blessing may abound for the Thessalonians. By *the Lord* he almost certainly means Jesus, but as we see from the preceding petition he makes no great distinction between the Father and the Son. For him, both were God, and were in some sense one. His prayer is for spiritual enlargement for his friends, and more particularly for enlargement in love. The two verbs *increase* and *abound* are more or less synonyms, the second being the stronger. Together they constitute a petition for the most abundant blessing. Some would understand *increase* as a reference to numerical increase, but this is not the meaning of the apostle. Rather the two verbs are to be taken together, and the following *in love* goes with both.

It is characteristic of the Christian outlook that Paul's prayer is for his friends to abound *in love one toward another, and toward all men*. Neil comments that, while love for each other was 'no more than the Gentiles practised', love for all men was more difficult and 'could only come as a gift from God'. But the specifically Christian quality of *agapē* is never natural to man, and comes only to him who has been transformed by the power of God. Whether it is exercised towards believers or non-believers, *agapē* is the gift of God. This, indeed, is implied in the fact that Paul makes it a matter for prayer. He is of course himself well aware that, if he would teach others, he himself must first practise the virtues which he urges upon them. Quite often, therefore, in these Epistles he is able to appeal to the example he and his companions were setting or had set. So here he affirms that they already exercised towards the Thessalonians the love of which he speaks.

13. The purpose of this abounding in love is now given. The verb *stablish* is used in verse 2 (where see note). In the Old Testament it is also combined with 'heart,' as in Ps. civ. 15, cxii. 8. 'Heart' here, as in ii. 4, does not refer simply to the emotional side of man's nature, as in our use of the term, but is the comprehensive term for the whole inner nature, including thought, feeling and willing. It stands for the whole personality. Paul's thought is that the whole personality of man can be established, strengthened, settled, given a sure confidence, only when there is a basis of abundant love. If the centre of a man's life is himself, then at best he will have an element of weakness and instability. But where he has learned to love the Lord his God with all his heart, and his neighbour as himself, then he has a firm foundation for life.

The *holiness* of which Paul speaks is the state of sanctity rather than the process of becoming holy (*hagiōsunē*, not *hagiasmos*). In the Greek Old Testament this word is used only of God; it is clear that it is the very highest degree of holiness that Paul desires for his friends. This is reinforced by *before God*. It is quite possible for a man to have high moral standards, and even, humanly speaking, to be blameless, and yet not to be holy. This, in fact, was what Paul himself had been in his pre-Christian days (see Phil. iii. 6 where his word for 'blameless,' *amemptos*, is the one he uses here). Holiness has an essential God-ward reference; it denotes the quality of being set apart for God, and the Christian should display it in pre-eminent measure.

Paul reinforces this by reminding them of the second coming of the Lord, and adds 'with all his holy ones' (AV *saints*). Exactly who these 'holy ones' are is not easy to see. As we have just said, the word 'holiness' in the Bible denotes being set apart for God, and as that is a characteristic of all who believe, the usual name for believers is simply 'holy ones' or 'saints'. In the New Testament 'saints' are not people who have won the special approbation of the Church because of their outstanding goodness; they are ordinary Church-members. But it does not seem likely that the term means ordinary Church-members in this particular context for it is to such people that these words are addressed, and the 'holy ones' in question will be coming to them at the Parousia.

Two suggestions are offered. 'Holy ones' may be angels (cf. Mk. viii. 38), or they may be the saints who have departed this life (cf. iv. 14).

In favour of the former identification is the fact that angels seem sometimes to be meant by the expression 'the holy ones' in the Scriptures of the Old Testament which were familiarly used by Paul (see Ps. lxxxix. 5; Dn. iv. 13 (Th.), viii. 13; Zc. xiv. 5). Further, angels are more than once associated with the Lord at His coming again (Mt. xiii. 41, xxv. 31; Mk. viii. 38; Lk. ix. 26; 2 Thes. i. 7). On the other hand, angels never seem to be referred to simply as 'the holy ones' in the New Testament. There the term almost invariably refers to men (albeit men here on earth, 'the saints'). In view of 1 Thes. iv. 14, 1 Cor. vi. 2, etc., it is clear that at the Parousia there will be believers associated with their Lord. Probably it is best to think of the term here as including both; after all Paul refers to '*all* his holy ones' and there seems nothing to indicate that the term is being restricted to one particular class.

V. EXHORTATION TO CHRISTIAN LIVING (iv. 1-12)
(a) General (iv. 1, 2)

As is usual in the Pauline writings we come to an exhortation to godly living towards the end of the Epistle. Here it is introduced by *Furthermore then*, a colloquial expression used to mark a transition, especially towards the conclusion of an argument. Phillips renders 'to sum up', but this is not the thought; 'finally' of RV and RSV is better. Perhaps 'for the rest' will give us the sense of it.

Paul begins by reminding the Thessalonians that they already had been told how they should live out their Christian faith. The New Testament writers often refer to the Christian life as a 'walk', and by so doing draw attention to the need for steady progress. The word for *ought* (*dei*='must') is a strong one; pleasing God is not a matter of personal choice, but an imperative necessity for the Christian. For *received* see on 1 Thes. ii. 13 (*paralambanō*) and for *please* on 1 Thes. ii. 4.

Paul proceeds to urge the Thessalonians to act on the

knowledge they had received. *Beseech* has reference to asking in the sense of requesting; *exhort* has the sense of urging or encouraging. *By the Lord Jesus* is really 'in the Lord Jesus', and it is basic to the whole exhortation. Paul does not presume to urge a line of conduct upon them because of his personal status or knowledge, but because he is in Christ, as they are, and this is the kind of conduct that should characterize those in Christ.

The same truth is insisted upon in verse 2, where Paul reminds them that the commands he had given were *by the Lord Jesus*. The preposition this time is *dia*,' through', which makes it quite clear that the commands in question were not Paul's, but God's (they came *through* Jesus). The meaning is basically much the same as in verse 1. Perhaps 'in the Lord Jesus' is more dynamic. But the repetition of the idea makes it clear that Paul is not concerned with merely human directions. He had, from the beginning, shown them the way of God, and this is what he continues to do. So confident is he that his message has all along been the same that he feels able to call the Thessalonians to witness, *ye know what commandments we gave you*. They could vouch that his directions had been consistent.

The word for *commandments* (*parangelia*) is not common in Christian writings, being found with reference to commands in the faith only in 1 Tim. i. 5, 18 (though the cognate verb is found more often). Properly it signifies an instruction passed on from one to another, as when a command is passed along a line of soldiers, and it is often used for military orders. It is thus very appropriate for authoritative commands, such as these given 'by authority of the Lord Jesus' (Moffatt).

The purpose of the apostle's request and exhortation is that the Thessalonians *would abound more and more*. We have already met this word *abound* in iii. 12 where it is used of abounding *in love*. Here, however, it is used absolutely, with no specific indication of the direction which the abounding is to take. The general use of the term brings before us the thought that the Christian life is the more abundant life (cf. Jn. x. 10). It is the only life which frees men.

(b) Sexual purity (iv. 3–8)

A marked feature of life in the first century Roman Empire, and more particularly in Greece, was the tendency to sexual laxity. The environment of the Thessalonian Christians was one in which men, as a rule, thought little of the sin involved in fornication. They accepted it simply as part of normal life, so much so that ritual fornication played a part in the worship of more than one deity, and men in general found it difficult to feel deeply on the subject.

But in this, as in many other things, the Christian faith refused to take its standards from contemporary society. It insisted that sexual vice incurs the wrath of God and is to be avoided scrupulously by every follower of the Christ. This is a lesson which is certainly not out of date, since the age in which we live is also one which is not conspicuous for high moral standards. As Neil trenchantly puts it, 'In our own semi-pagan society, it needs to be stated again as firmly as Paul does here. "Affairs" are not a source of easy laughs for radio or variety comedians, but—more properly described as promiscuous fornication—are one of the Seven Deadly Sins.'

3. Paul puts the whole matter on the highest plane by his opening remark, *this is the will of God*. In the Greek *will* has no article, signifying that what follows is not the whole will of God. There are, of course, many other things that God wills that we should do or not do; but that will includes within it the injunction which follows. Christian man must not concern himself only with those things which appeal to him. He must have regard to the fact that God is interested in all that he does, and God's will is that he should be pure. *Sanctification* signifies the process of which *holiness* is the completed state. From the moment a man believes he becomes set apart for God, or 'holy' in the New Testament terminology; he is a 'saint'. As we saw in our note on iii. 13 this does not mean that he is morally perfect, but that he is given over to God to do His will. Thus a process is begun in which the old ways and the old habits are increasingly done away and replaced with new ways which fit in with the service of God. This is a long process but a very necessary one, and much of the New Testament is taken up with instruction as to how it may be furthered. Here Paul lays it down firmly that it is God's will that His people should live in this way.

The particular aspect of sanctification which is in mind here is sexual purity, and Paul immediately goes on to define it first negatively and then positively. Negatively, *that ye should abstain from fornication*, where he emphasizes the thought of separation by the use of the preposition *apo*. The Christian must keep himself far from this evil thing. As Phillips translates, 'and that entails first of all a clean cut with sexual immorality'.

4. Then, positively, each should keep himself in sanctification and honour. It is interesting to find the verb *know* used in this connection (there is no *how* in the Greek; the verse runs 'that each of you should know to possess. . . .'). It is as though the sin is unthinkable in one who knows what his Christian faith implies. This is capable of wider application, and it is always good for Christ's followers to enter more completely into a knowledge of what their faith means in terms of daily life. Paul uses the word *sanctification* again, for such mastery of self is to be looked for in those who walk the way of holiness. With this he links *honour*, for sexual impurity brings only dishonour and shame.

There is a problem as to the meaning of *vessel* (Gk. *skeuos*). Most of the early Greek commentators took it to mean 'body', although *skeuos* is not found elsewhere with this meaning. This interpretation is supported by the partial parallels in 2 Cor. iv. 7 and similar passages, and by the fact that, in Greek writers generally, the body is sometimes thought of as the instrument or container of the soul. Theodore of Mopsuestia, Augustine and others, however, thought of the word here as meaning 'wife'[1] (so Moffatt, 'to take a wife for himself'). This view is supported by the fact that the verb *possess*, which literally means 'acquire', is not very suitable for 'body', but

[1] *Keli*, the Hebrew equivalent of *skeuos*, is used in Rabbinic writings of the wife. See Strack-Billerbeck, *in loc.*

is found in the Septuagint and elsewhere of marrying a wife. Again, in 1 Pet. iii. 7 the wife is spoken of as 'the weaker vessel.' This last point however does not count for much, for (a) both husband and wife are 'vessels' in this verse, the wife being the 'weaker', and (b) both are vessels of the Holy Ghost; the wife is not spoken of as the husband's 'vessel'.

The big difficulty in the way of 'body' is the verb 'acquire', and the big difficulty in the way of 'wife' is that this points to a very low view of marriage (i.e. that the primary function of the wife is to satisfy her husband's sexual desires), just where the apostle is advocating a high view. The point may perhaps be decided by the fact that the verb is found in the papyri in the sense 'possess' (Moulton-Milligan cite a papyrus dated A.D. 59 where one, Thoon, declares on oath that he 'has' thirty days to produce a man he has bailed out. They, however, take the view that in the Thessalonians passage the meaning is 'gradually obtain the complete mastery of the body'). Since this is so, it would seem better to take *vessel* as meaning 'body' and the sense of the verse as 'Keep your bodies pure'.

5. There is no connecting particle between this verse and the preceding one, so that the same thought is carried on. *Not in the lust of concupiscence.* The former of these two nouns, *pathos*, properly denotes 'a feeling which the mind suffers' (Grimm-Thayer), and so a passion. Findlay says it 'signifies not, like Eng. "passion", a violent feeling, but an overmastering feeling, in which the man is borne along by evil as though its passive instrument' (C.G.T.). It denotes the passive side of a vice whereas the following word *epithumia* is concerned with the active side. (See on ii. 17, where it is translated *desire*.) The combination has a meaning like 'the passion of lust' (RV), and indicates the surrender of a man to his passions.

We have already indicated that this surrender was common enough in the world of that day, and Paul goes on to point out that it was, in fact, characteristic of *the Gentiles.* This word usually denotes the non-Jewish nations, but sometimes, as here, it signifies those outside the Christian Church. Their characteristic is that they *know not God*. This does not mean that God had given them no revelation of Himself, but that, in the manner detailed at greater length in Romans i. 18ff., they had rejected the light that they had, and so could be said to have no true knowledge of God. Paul has in mind not an innocent ignorance but blameworthy neglect of the revelation given to them, so that, in consequence, they were given up to unnatural lusts (cf. Rom. i. 24ff.). It is still true that much unbelief has its basis in a rejection of the light that God has given.

6. *That no man go beyond* . . . is probably to be understood as 'so that no man . . . ', indicating the result of obedience to the injunction of verses 3, 4. The literal meaning of the verb *huperbainō* is 'to go beyond', and thus 'to go beyond bounds', 'to transgress'; but where it has a personal object it may signify 'to overreach' (Moffatt 'defraud'). *Pleonekteō* is literally 'to have more', and comes to mean intransitively 'to have an advantage', 'to excel', and transitively 'to take advantage of another'. This, in view of the object *his brother*, will be its meaning here. The flow of the sentence may mean that the former verb is likewise to be taken as transitive (though RSV renders 'that no man transgress, and wrong his brother'). There is some question as to the exact reference here, for *huperbainō* is quite general in its meaning, and *pleonekteō* is naturally associated with covetousness and avarice. AV apparently takes it as general, for it renders the following words *in any matter*. But the Greek is literally 'in the matter'. This use of the definite article seems to make it plain that Paul is continuing the thought of the previous verse, and not introducing a new topic. This is strengthened by the fact that uncleanness is referred to in the following verse, so that the idea of impurity continues through this verse and beyond. The meaning, then, is that sexual sin, besides being an offence against holiness and honour, is an act of fraud against a *brother*, in taking what is rightly his. *Brother* in this sense does not, of course, mean 'a brother in Christ', but 'a brother man'. What Paul is saying properly applies to impure relations after marriage; but the same principle applies to pre-marital promiscuity. For the impure person cannot bring to the marriage that virginity which is the other's due.

A salutary reminder follows that such conduct cannot go unpunished. *Avenger* means 'one who satisfies justice', i.e. by punishing the wrongdoer (cf. Rom. xiii. 4). *Of all such* (better 'concerning all these things') indicates that God will punish breaches of all the sins referred to, namely all sins of uncleanness. This probably looks forward to the Day of Judgment, though there is a sense in which God's judgment operates in the present (as in Rom. i. 24, 26, 28). This also was part of Paul's original preaching at Thessalonica, and he insists that the preachers had 'solemnly testified' to this (the compound verb means more than *testified*).

7. The solemnity of this warning is now underlined with a reminder of the whole purpose of the Christian life, a life which rests on the basis of a divine call, not on human initiative. The divine will is primary in Christian life. The idea of the calling of God does not feature largely in the Thessalonian Epistles, but it is undoubtedly there. From the time of his own spectacular conversion Paul was in no doubt that the primary fact is that God calls men, and not that men decide to be God's people, and it is of interest to see this major Pauline conception making its appearance in these early letters (see also ii. 12, v. 24; 2 Thes. ii. 14).

There is a change of preposition in this verse. *Unto* (*epi*) *uncleanness* gives the idea of purpose, of being called 'for'. We see the word used, for example, in Gal. v. 13 of being called *unto liberty*, and in Eph. ii. 10 of being created *unto good works*. God's purpose in calling the Christian was not that he should live in *uncleanness*. The preposition with *holiness* is *en* (cf. *in newness of life*, Rom. vi. 4). Christians are called so that they shall be 'in holiness' or rather, 'in sanctification', the word used being the one descriptive of the process as in verse 3, and not that referring to the state as in iii. 13.

8. This argument is carried a step further by pointing out that the man who sins in this way really sins against the Holy Spirit. *Therefore* points us to a consequence. Because God has called us in sanctification it follows that those who treat this lightly are despising no less a person than God Himself.

There is some difficulty about the word *atheteō*, rendered *despiseth*. Elsewhere it is rendered 'rejected' (Lk. vii. 30), 'frustrate' (Gal. ii. 21), 'bring to nothing' (1 Cor. i. 19). It means something like 'to treat as null and void', 'to regard as of no account', and this is its significance here. The person who regards sexual sin so lightly, as something which does not matter greatly, is, in effect, treating God as One who can be disregarded, for the prohibition we are considering is of divine and not human origin. For a somewhat similar thought see Lk. x. 16.

The particular aspect of the divine activity that is singled out for mention in this connection is that God gives the Holy Spirit. AV reads *who hath also given*, but the better manuscripts have the participle in the present. It is not that the offenders despise a God who once gave the Spirit; they offend against a gift proffered at the moment of their sin, against the continuing presence of the Spirit. Paul often thinks of the Spirit as given in the past, i.e. at the beginning of a man's spiritual life (see e.g., Gal. iv. 6), but the thought here is like that of 1 Cor. vi. 19 (where also the warning is against fornication) 'What? know ye not that your body is the temple of the Holy Ghost which is in you, which ye have of God?'

Two further touches remain for mention. In referring to the Holy Spirit Paul uses an expression which is literally 'the Spirit of Him the Holy', which is a stronger and more stately expression than that usually employed, and one which emphasizes both the majesty of Him with whom we have to do, and the holiness which is so much a feature of this passage. The other is that he speaks of the Spirit as being given to 'you' (not *us* as AV), thus removing the statement from the sphere of the general, and making it personal to the Thessalonians.

(c) Brotherly love (iv. 9, 10)

9. Two things in particular marked off the Christian Church of New Testament days from contemporary society; the purity of the lives of its members, and the love that they so fully practised. Here we find Paul passing from the one to the other. *Brotherly love* (*philadelphia*) is not the same as love in general (*agapē*). This latter is the attitude of benevolence toward all which must characterize those who have experienced the *agapē* of God (see on i. 3). Love such as this should be exercised by the Christian toward all men, including fellow-Christians, irrespective of their merit or lack of merit. He should also exercise a special *brotherly love* toward those in the household of faith. Outside the New Testament the word *philadelphia* almost invariably denotes the love binding together the children of one father; in the New Testament it is without exception used for the love uniting Christians to one another. James Denney thought that the importance of this 'is not sufficiently considered by most Christian people; who, if they looked into the matter, might find that few of their strongest affections were determined by the common faith. Is not love a strong and peculiar word to describe the feeling you cherish toward some members of the Church, brethren to you in Christ Jesus? yet love to the brethren is the very token of our right to a place in the Church for ourselves.' These words are not yet out of date.

Paul assures his friends that there is no need for him to exhort them in this matter (cf. his words in 2 Cor. viii. 1ff.), and gives as the reason for it that they were *taught of God to love one another*. *Theodidaktoi* (*taught of God*) occurs only here in the New Testament. It points to an activity of God within their heart, and follows strikingly on the reference to the work of the Holy Spirit in the previous verse. We are reminded of the words of our Lord in Jn. vii. 17, 'if any man will do his will, he shall know of the doctrine'. Where there is a genuine yielding to God for the doing of His will, there a man is *taught of God*.

10. *And indeed* marks an advance on the preceding statement. It is one thing to know what to do, and another to do it; but the Thessalonians were conspicuous for the way in which they practised love of the brethren. The present *ye do* has its full force of continuous action 'ye habitually do it'. *All Macedonia.* In this province we know of churches only at Philippi, Beroea and Thessalonica; but that need not mean that only these three existed. The believers in these centres would spread the gospel, and missionaries like Silvanus, Timothy and Luke had been active in the area. Lightfoot thought it probable that churches had been established at least in the larger towns like Amphipolis and Pella. But Paul would not have them rest on their oars. He therefore urges *that ye increase more and more*. The verb *increase* is that rendered *abound* in iii. 12, iv. 1 (where see notes). In this section of the Epistle Paul comes back repeatedly to the thought of the abundant life. Although the primary meaning here is of abounding in love, yet we may comment that growth and freedom from constricting restraints are integral parts of the Christian experience.

(d) Earning one's living (iv. 11, 12)

11. Phillips renders the opening words 'and to make it your ambition to have no ambition!' which reproduces something of the vigorous paradox employed by the apostle. Following the injunction to abound in love of one another he exhorts them to take a lowly place. The exact meaning of his words is not completely clear, for the verb *philotimeomai* can be understood in more ways than one. In the classics it meant 'to be ambitious', but in later Greek came to signify 'to strive eagerly', 'to seek restlessly', and signified a wholehearted and energetic pursuit of the object. In both its other New Testament occurrences (Rom. xv. 20; 2 Cor. v. 9) it has the latter meaning, and it seems likely that this is also its sense in the present passage in accordance with the general meaning of the verb in late Greek. But, whether we understand it as 'make it your ambition to be unambitious' or 'seek restlessly to be still', it makes a colourful statement.

Also depending on the imperative 'seek restlessly' are the two following infinitives *to do your own business, and to work with your own hands*. Why this stress on the virtues of the quiet life, and of steadily working at one's occupation? There is evidence that some of the Thessalonians were rather restless and, in view of what they believed to be the near approach of the Parousia, were not doing any work (cf. 2 Thes. iii. 11). It is not unlikely that it was such people Paul had specially in mind when giving these strong injunctions to avoid the spectacular and to work hard.

It is noteworthy that he particularizes and says *work with your own hands*. Among the Greeks manual labour was little esteemed. In strong contrast with the attitude of the Jews, it was regarded as the occupation of a slave. In this matter Christianity did not hesitate to insist on the dignity of manual labour (cf. Eph. iv. 28). Some have seen in these words an indication that the majority of the Thessalonians were of the artisan class, and this may well have been so. There are few indications throughout the two Epistles that any of them were at all wealthy; rather everything points to their coming from the lower strata of society.

This was the reiteration of a command that Paul had already given them. In reminding them of it he uses a verb often employed in the classics of the orders of military officers. There is a ring of authority about it.

12. Two reasons are given for thus earning their own living. First, *that ye may walk honestly toward them that are without. Honestly* is used in its older English sense, 'in a seemly manner', 'becomingly'. In one sense the Christian must live without regard to the opinion of the world, for his standards are those of his Master, and not those of the community in which he lives. But in another sense he must always think of the effect of his actions on other people, and must take care not to bring discredit on the faith by being careless of appearances. The Thessalonians, as we have seen, were distinguished by 'love of the brethren', and this, apparently, was so strong that some of them had been able to stop working for their living and were subsisting on the bounty of others. This may have been a testimony to the charity of those who provided for them; but the effect on outsiders would be deplorable, and thus Paul counsels them to act carefully.

The second reason he gives is that they may be independent. The Greek is equally capable of being rendered 'that you may have need of nothing', and 'that you may have need of no man', either giving a good sense. If some were living on the charity of others they needed to be told to be independent of men. Or the words may indicate that the man who works constantly will find ample provision for all his needs. He will have no lack. The grammatical point, that the Greek for 'have need of' is usually followed by a thing rather than a person, may be the decisive consideration, and thus we accept the meaning as given in the AV.

VI. PROBLEMS ASSOCIATED WITH THE PAROUSIA
(iv. 13—v. 11)
(a) Believers who died before the Parousia (iv. 13-18)

Paul had clearly spoken about the Parousia[1] to good effect, and the Thessalonians were in no doubt that it would take place. But equally clearly he had not been able to deal with all the problems associated with it, some of which obviously came up after his departure. One of them has been dealt with in the preceding section, namely the manner in which men should occupy themselves during the interval. Now he turns his attention to another difficulty.

It would seem that some, at least, of the Thessalonians had understood him to say that all who believed would see the Parousia; but now some believers had died and they had begun to wonder about them. Did this mean that they would be at some disadvantage when the Lord came? Had they forfeited their share in the wonderful happenings of the End? Some may even have felt that these deaths discredited the whole idea of the Parousia. Incidentally, the fact that such a question could be asked indicates that we are dealing with an early writing, for the question was bound to arise early in the Church's history.

[1]For this term see notes on 1 Thes. ii. 19.

13. *I would not have you to be ignorant* is a formula used by Paul on a number of occasions, always accompanied by the affectionate *brethren*, and drawing attention to some point which is important, and which may be new to them (cf. Rom. i. 13, xi. 25; 1 Cor. x. 1, xii. 1; 2 Cor. i. 8).

He speaks of the departed as 'them who are falling asleep' (rather than *them which are asleep*), using the present participle, a construction which indicates a present happening and which also implies the future awakening more definitely than the more usual perfect would have done. Although among Jews and even pagans death is sometimes likened to sleep, it is a particularly apt metaphor for Christians to use since for them the whole concept of death has been transformed. (In passing we note that 'cemetery', *koimēterion*, is derived from the word used here, *koimaō*, and means 'a place of sleep'.)

That ye sorrow not, even as others has sometimes been taken as indicating that Christians may sorrow, but not in the same degree as heathen. This seems to be straining the Greek. We need not doubt that a certain sadness at parting is natural and inevitable; but Paul here 'states his precept broadly, without caring to enter into the qualifications which will suggest themselves at once to thinking men' (Lightfoot).

Others which have no hope is a general term for the whole non-Christian world, and the characterization is peculiarly apt. Pagan literature reveals a hopelessness in the face of death which is matched by the inscriptions on tombs. The contrast between the pagan and the Christian attitude to death is exemplified in two early statements which Frame cites. The first is a letter of the second century and reads:

'Irene to Taonnophris and Philo, good comfort. I was as sorry and wept over the departed one as I wept for Didymas. And all things whatsoever were fitting, I did, and all mine, Epaphroditus and Thermuthion and Philion and Apollonius and Plantas. But, nevertheless, against such things one can do nothing. Therefore comfort ye one another'.

The second is from a Christian of about the same date, Aristides.

> 'And if any righteous man among them passes from the world, they rejoice and offer thanks to God; and they escort the body as if he were setting out from one place to another near'.

There are some noble pagan utterances on immortality; but they are by no means typical, and probably had not penetrated through to ordinary people, so that the contrast between the two passages here quoted may fairly be taken as representative.

14. The reason for the Christian certainty is the divine action in Christ's death and resurrection. The Christian view of death is not the result of some speculative philosophical theory, but of God's intervention to bring about man's salvation; and because it is the divine action it allows of no doubts. Thus Paul here directs the attention of the Thessalonians to the central doctrines of their faith. It is significant that he does not speak of Christ 'sleeping' but uses the word *died*. He died that death which is the wages of sin; and because He endured the full horror implied in that death, He has transformed death for His followers into sleep.[1]

The end of this verse reads literally 'them that sleep through Jesus will God bring'. It is uncertain what 'through Jesus' means, and whether it should be taken with the preceding or the following words. Moffatt and RSV take it with *will bring;* but the parallelism of the sentence is against this view, as are the necessity for showing that not all the dead are meant, and the fact that in verse 16 we read of *the dead in Christ*. Moreover it is a rather tame, and even redundant ending to say 'God will bring through Jesus with Jesus. . . .' It seems preferable then to take 'through Jesus' with 'them that sleep'. But 'sleeping through Jesus' is not a very easy idea (this being the chief reason why some adopt the alternative view), and our best understanding of it is that death has been transformed into

---

[1] The subject of death is dealt with at greater length in my monograph *The Wages of Sin* (Tyndale Press, 1955).

sleep through Jesus. Whereas for the natural man death is the antagonist which no man can combat, for the Christian it is completely without terrors (cf. 1 Cor. xv. 54–57). For him it is no more than sleep, the transformation being effected, Paul says, 'through Jesus'.

The concluding *with him* is taken by some commentators to mean that Christ will lead them to glory (Lightfoot, Frame, etc.). But, true though this is, it does not seem to be the meaning of this verse. Rather, Paul is concerned with Christ bringing them with Him at His Parousia. The Thessalonians do not seem to have doubted the reality of the resurrection (Paul says *will bring*, not 'will raise'); but they had to be reassured of the place in the Parousia of the faithful departed. Paul gives the conclusion a touch of certainty. After *if we believe* we expect 'even so also we ought to believe . . . ', but Paul states it not as a matter of belief or obligation, but of fact.

15. When he comes to the declaration for which the Thessalonians were looking, Paul makes his words as authoritative as possible by saying that he speaks *by the word of the Lord*. The most natural interpretation of this is that he is quoting a saying of Jesus; but a difficulty is that there is no saying in the Gospels which exactly meets the case (Mt. xxiv. 31 being perhaps the closest). There is nothing improbable in the hypothesis that Paul is quoting an otherwise unrecorded saying, for Jesus must have said many things which have not been included in the canonical Gospels (cf. Acts xx. 35). Again we cannot rule out the possibility of some direct revelation to the apostle. Possible, but not quite so likely, is the hypothesis that he means that this is the result of his pondering of the problem under the guidance of the Holy Spirit, in accordance with his claim in 1 Cor. ii. 16 to have 'the mind of Christ' (cf. also ii. 13).

The question that is raised by the words *we which are alive . . .* is whether Paul means that he expects to be alive himself when the Lord returns. While there is nothing unlikely in the idea that Paul thought the Parousia would take place in his own lifetime, yet it must be borne in mind that he consistently refused to commit himself to dates, and indeed, a few verses later on he speaks as though he did not know when it would occur (v. 1, 2). The words he uses here, while congruous with the idea that he thought that he himself would be among those who would survive to that day, are not strong enough to establish it, and the meaning may be given in Lightfoot's paraphrase, 'When I say "we", I mean those who are living, those who survive to that day.'[1] These will certainly not (emphatic negative *ou mē*, found only four times in Paul outside quotations from the LXX) precede (this is the meaning of the Old English *prevent*) those who have fallen asleep.

16. 'One word of command, one shout from the Archangel, one blast from the trumpet of God and God in Person will come down from heaven!' This translation of Phillips catches something of the vividness of the sequence of events outlined. This is the fullest description of the Parousia in the New Testament, and when we reflect on the little that is said here we are warned against being unduly dogmatic about what will then happen. Paul's main point is that it is none other than the Lord Himself who will come. The end of the age is not to be ushered in by some intermediary, but by God Himself (cf. Mic. i. 3). The whole scene is awe-inspiring and full of grandeur.

The *shout* (*keleusma*) is a word of command, and is used of the shout of the charioteer to his horses or the hunter to his hounds. It is the cry to the rowers uttered by the ship's master, or to soldiers by their commander. Always there is the ring of authority and the note of urgency. It is not said who will utter the shout, but very likely it is the Lord. If not, then it is possible that the *shout*, the *voice* and the *trump* are three ways of referring to the same thing (cf. Rev. i. 10ff. for a voice like the sound of a trumpet). Some have tried to particularize the

---

[1] In passing we note that those are surely wrong who affirm that Paul thought of the Parousia as imminent during his early years, but that the idea faded in later life. Phil. iv. 5 shows that, much later, he still thought of the Lord's coming as at hand.

archangel, and Michael, the only archangel named in the New Testament, is usually favoured (Gabriel is often ranked with Michael, but in Lk. i. 19, 26 he is called simply an 'angel'). But *archangelou* in the Greek is without the article and it would seem that Paul has no particular archangel in view here. Similarly *voice* is anarthrous, and the meaning thus is 'a voice of an archangel', or perhaps even 'a voice like an archangel's'.

The trumpet is mentioned twice in 1 Cor. xv. 52, and Paul clearly regarded it as having a special place in the sequence of events at the Parousia. Cf. Ex. xix. 16; Is. xxvii. 13; Joel ii. 1; Zc. ix. 14 for Old Testament passages associating the sound of the trumpet with divine activity, and Mt. xxiv. 31 for the same in the teaching of the Lord. Klausner says that the idea existed in Judaism at this time.[1]

The dead in Christ are to be first to rise, i.e. before the events in the next verse. It is unlikely that Paul has here in mind the *first resurrection* of Rev. xx. 5, or that he is thinking of the resurrection of all men. All that he is doing is pointing out that, far from the faithful departed missing the Parousia, they will have a prominent place.

17. Then, after they have risen to be with Christ, those believers who remain will be *caught up together with them in the clouds*. The verb *harpagēsometha* combines the ideas of force and suddenness. It denotes the irresistible power of God. That they will be caught up *together with* the faithful departed should not be overlooked. It will be a reunion with Christ; but it will also be a reunion with the friends who have gone before. The majesty of the whole scene is emphasized with the setting 'in clouds' (cf. Dn. vii. 13; Mt. xxiv. 30, xxvi. 64; Rev. i. 7). There they will *meet the Lord in the air*. The air was usually thought to be the abode of all manner of evil spirits (cf. Eph. ii. 2), and it is thus a measure of the complete supremacy of the Lord that He should meet His saints in such a region. At the same time this is not being spoken of as anything more

[1] *From Jesus to Paul*, London, 1946, pp. 538f.

than a meeting place. The impression we obtain is that the Lord proceeds to the earth with His people (cf. 1 Cor. vi. 2).

The climax is reached with *so shall we ever be with the Lord.* There are doubtless many points on which we should like further information; but when Paul comes to that great fact, which includes everything else, and makes everything else unimportant, he ceases. There is nothing to add to it.

18. Paul calls on them not simply to take heart, but actively to exhort or comfort each other (for *parakaleō* see on iii. 2) with the words that he has written. They represent a source of continual strengthening to the believer, for they give the assurance that the power of God will never be defeated. The Christian will find himself in difficulties; but he knows that God is over all, and that when He sees that the time has come, this age will draw to its close, and the Parousia will usher in that new age wherein His supremacy will be manifest to all. Whether we live, or whether we die, we do not go beyond His power; and in the face of death, that antagonist no man can master, we can yet remain calm and triumphant, for we know that those who sleep sleep in Jesus, and that there is a place for them in the final scheme of things. Well might Paul call on his friends to *comfort one another with these words.*

(b) The time of the Parousia (v. 1–3)

A second difficulty about the Parousia now claims attention. It would seem that some of the Thessalonians, thinking of the position of the faithful departed in relation to the Parousia, had begun to wonder what their own position was to be. If only the living were to have a part in the happenings of the great day, then they too might be cut off by death, and so fail to participate. How could they know when the end would be? Their difficulty has been met already in Paul's answer to the former difficulty, but he proceeds to give attention to the matter of date.

1. His first point is that they really have no need for instruction in the matter of the time. He had spoken of this in his first preaching, and evidently counted on this as having been well learned at the time, so that he had no need to write on the topic. He makes use of two words for 'times', the first, *chronoi*, denoting time in its chronological aspect as mere succession, and the second, *kairoi* (*seasons*), having reference rather to time in its qualitative aspect. Thus if a young man spends five minutes with his fiancée the chronological time is exactly the same as when he spends five minutes in the dentist's chair, but the quality of the two periods is different. He may well feel that the former is but a fleeting moment, and the latter not much short of eternity! With regard to the second advent, then, the *chronoi* are the chronological epochs that must elapse, time considered simply with regard to its duration, while the *kairoi* focus our attention rather on the nature of the times, on the critical events which will take place as heralding the coming of the Lord.

In thinking thus of the great future events the affectionate address *brethren* is employed.

2. The opening *yourselves* reminds the Thessalonians that the answer to this particular difficulty was within their grasp if they but reflected on what they already knew. Findlay finds the word *perfectly* puzzling here; taking it to mean 'precisely', he thinks it must have been used in a letter from the Thessalonians, and that Paul is taking up and repeating their word. The Greek *akribōs* does connect with the idea of accuracy (cf. its use in Lk. i. 3, where it is rendered 'perfect'), but the right explanation of its use here seems rather to be that there was nothing to add to what they already knew on the subject. There may also be a hint that their information was ultimately based on some word of the Lord like Mt. xxiv. 43; Lk. xii. 39 (cf. 2 Pet. iii. 10).

The day of the Lord is an Old Testament idea, going back to Amos. He, however, uses the term as already well-known, and opposes the accepted understanding of it in his day that it would be a time of judgment on the heathen, pointing out that Israel, too, would be judged. However, it would seem that the old idea lingered on, and many looked for the day when the enemies of Israel would be destroyed. In the New Testament the Day is associated with Christ as well as with the Father (Phil. i. 6, etc.), and it is referred to under a variety of names. The idea of judgment remained (indeed, 'day of judgment' is one of the ways of referring to it, as in 2 Pet. ii. 9), but the emphasis is on individual judgment, rather than judgment of the nations, and the truth is insisted upon that 'every one of us shall give account of himself to God' (Rom. xiv. 12). Here neither *day* nor *Lord* has the article, which indicates that the expression was regarded much as a proper noun. There is also a certain stress on the character of the day as belonging to the Lord, rather than the denoting of a definite day.

The present tense *cometh* makes the sentence more vivid. The comparison to the coming of a thief indicates its total unexpectedness. The addition of *in the night* is found only here, being absent in the better manuscripts from similar passages like 2 Pet. iii. 10 (cf. RV).

3. Absent also from the better manuscripts is the opening *For*, so that, since there is no connecting particle, this verse stands in the closest connection with the preceding. The subject of the verb is not defined, but clearly it is unbelievers in general who will be thinking that all is at peace. The verb is in the present subjunctive in the Greek which signifies that they will be saying these things at the moment that doom comes upon them. *Peace* reminds us of Ezk. xiii. 10; Je. vi. 14, viii. 11; Mi. iii. 5, and to it is added a fairly rare word for *safety* (once each in Luke and Acts in the rest of the New Testament).

When men are in this fancied security, while they are actually saying *peace*, there will come on them *sudden destruction*. Again we have the verb in the present for greater vividness. There are a number of coincidences of language with Lk. xxi. 34 (such as the unusual word *aiphnidios*, *sudden*, found in these two places only in the New Testament), and this is not the only place wherein Paul agrees with Luke in statements where that evangelist differs from the others. It indicates a connection such as we should expect between Paul and his friend.

The *destruction* spoken of is probably to be understood primarily in terms of separation from God (cf. 2 Thes. i. 9 where the same word is used), rather than annihilation. Milligan understands by it 'the thought of utter and hopeless *ruin*, the loss of all that gives worth to existence'. The comparison with child-birth can be paralleled from the Old Testament (Is. xiii. 6–8; Je. iv. 31, etc.), and from the teaching of our Lord (Mk. xiii. 8). Sometimes the point of the comparison is the pain, but here it is rather a combination of suddenness and inevitability, the latter point being underlined by the following *they shall not escape*.

(c) Children of the day (v. 4–11)

In strong contrast with the fate of these unbelievers is the situation of those in Christ (the *ye* is emphatic). The apostle makes use of a word play wherein the day of the Lord passes into the day or light in which Christians live, and he develops the thought of living as children of the day.

4. Paul expresses his confidence that the Thessalonians would not find themselves in the calamitous situation he has just outlined. 'You', he says, 'are no longer dwellers in darkness.' Since they have come into the light of Christ they have passed from the possibility of such destruction. *That day* is clearly the day of judgment just referred to. It seems likely that he is carrying on the metaphor of the thief coming suddenly in the night. However some manuscripts have a reading which means 'as day overtakes thieves' (*kleptas* as against *kleptēs*), and this is accepted by Lightfoot, Milligan, Frame and others, largely on the grounds that scribes would not alter the accepted reading to this one, but they would be greatly tempted to make this one conform to the other. However the reading in AV has better manuscript attestation, and the variant is explicable as a mechanical corruption (the ending of *kleptēs* being conformed to the nearby *humas*). The sense of AV is better, and we adopt the accepted reading.

5. The reason for the day's not surprising them is given from its positive side, *ye are all the children* (lit. 'sons') *of light*. In the Semitic idiom to be a 'son' of something is to be characterized by that thing; so, when Christians are spoken of as 'sons of light', the meaning is that 'light' is their distinguishing characteristic. This is more than simply being 'in light'. 'Sons of day' is not simply a repetition of 'sons of light' but marks a slightly different thought. It is similar to 'sons of light', for day is the region of light; but it refers back also to *the day of the Lord*. Being 'sons of light' they are also 'sons of the day of the Lord' with all that that means in terms of participation in the triumph of that great day.

Next Paul exhorts his friends to right living in view of their character as those who will share in the blessings of the Parousia, and there is a significant change from *ye* to *we*, with the apostle associating himself with his friends in the need to observe the injunctions which follow. But first he points out that *we*, i.e. 'we who believe', do not belong to the sphere of night or darkness. *Night*, corresponding to *day*, is the period, and *darkness* (over against *light*) is the condition of opposition to God.

6. *Therefore* (*ara oun*) is a strong expression for a necessary logical inference, and introduces an inescapable conclusion. Paul uses a different word for *sleep* (*katheudō*) from that employed in iv. 13ff. (*koimaō*), and one which is elsewhere used of moral indifference (Mk. xiii. 36; Eph. v. 14). It is the condition natural to the enemies of Christ, for they belong to the night. They are referred to here as *others*, or 'the rest', i.e. all non-Christians.

By contrast with such people Christians are exhorted *let us watch and be sober*. *Watch* enjoins mental alertness and a remembrance of the second coming (cf. Christ's use of the term in Mt. xxiv. 42f., xxv. 13; Mk. xiii. 34ff., etc.), while *be sober* has rather a moral emphasis, and condemns all kinds of excess. Christians must live temperately. While the verb can be used of the avoidance of alcoholic intoxication, it is probable that its use here is metaphorical (as with *sleep* and *watch*), for there is no indication that the Thessalonians were addicted to drunkenness and thus in need of an exhortation to sobriety in the literal sense. Rather Paul is exhorting them to that temperance, which, avoiding excess of all kinds, leads to a balanced life.

7. The injunctions of the previous verse are reinforced by a reminder that the kind of conduct he is opposing properly belongs to the night, not the day, and he has already pointed out that his readers are 'sons of day'. It does not seem profitable to be seeking for metaphorical meanings for the expressions used here; what Paul is doing is saying that night is the time when men sleep and when they get drunk. He uses two different verbs in connection with the latter, the first of which means literally 'to get drunk' (in the passive: the active is 'to make drunk'), and the second 'to be drunk'. But there is no stress on the difference here, and Paul uses them virtually as synonyms, the variation being purely stylistic.

8. *But* (in contrast with such people) *let us, who are of the day, be sober*. The relative clause is our rendering of a participial construction which has something of a causal force, 'since we are of the day'. The injunction to sobriety is repeated, and this forms a transition to the idea of the armour of the Christian soldier. Just what is the connection of thought is not easy to see, but there is a similar sequence in Rom. xiii. 12f. Perhaps, as Lightfoot thought, 'the mention of vigilance suggested the idea of a sentry armed and on duty'. Paul uses an aorist participle for *putting on*, suggesting the taking of a decisive, once-for-all step.

The metaphor of armour is one which had a certain attraction for the apostle, for he uses it in Rom. xiii. 12f., 2 Cor. vi. 7, x. 4, and Eph. vi. 13ff., where the idea is most fully developed. The details are not always the same, which is a warning against pressing the metaphor too closely. Thus, in Ephesians, the breastplate is righteousness, while faith is the shield and neither hope nor love is mentioned. The whole idea probably goes back to Is. lix. 17, where Jehovah is depicted as a warrior armed.

Once again we find the great triad of faith, hope and love (see on i. 3), and once again we find hope coming last with a certain emphasis, which is natural in an Epistle which places so much stress on hope. The construction in each case gives us an appositional genitive, so that the breastplate consists of *faith and love*, and the helmet of *the hope of salvation*.

Salvation is the general and inclusive term for the whole great work of Christ achieved for man, of which redemption and the like are partial aspects. Here its being linked so definitely with hope brings us to the consideration that the aspect of salvation that is especially in mind is the future, eschatological aspect. The hope of the consummation of all things, wherein our Christian salvation will be fully revealed, is indeed a helmet for the Christian, warding off from him blows that otherwise would be fatal.

9. The reason for *the hope of salvation* is given as God's appointment. The word *appointed (etheto)* is 'somewhat vague' (Milligan), being not nearly as definite, for example, as 'predestinated' (Rom. viii. 29f., etc.); but it clearly makes our salvation rest primarily on the divine initiative. It is due to Him that Christian men are brought into a state of salvation.

Negatively Paul says that God did not appoint us *to wrath*, bringing before us once more the terrible fate of the lost (see on i. 10). It needs to be emphasized in these days that salvation is very much salvation *from* as well as salvation *unto*. As Heinrich Vogel puts it, 'whoever thinks he can smile at God's wrath will never praise him eternally for his grace'.[1] One of the things that gave salvation so full a meaning to New Testament Christians was that they were sure of the wrath of God, and knew that Christ had rescued them from a terrible fate. In modern days men are often prone to take Christianity lightly because they have emptied the wrath of its content.

[1] *The Iron Ration of a Christian*, London, 1941, p. 102.

To remove the wrath of God from the scene is to rob life of a good deal of its serious purpose.

There is a difference of opinion about the meaning of the expression *to obtain salvation* (*eis peripoiēsin sōtērias*), the alternatives being 'for the acquiring of salvation' and, taking the former word passively, 'for the adoption to salvation'. The question is whether Paul is saying that we obtain salvation, which might be held to make it to some extent a matter of human activity, or that God adopts us into salvation. The former seems to be the meaning of the word in 2 Thes. ii. 14, Heb. x. 39, and the latter in Eph. i. 14, 1 Pet. ii. 9. But though the passive meaning is found in these cases, the natural meaning of the verse is 'for the acquiring' or 'obtaining of salvation'. This, of course, does not mean that salvation is obtained by human effort, and Paul immediately goes on to say that it is obtained *by* (lit. 'through') *our Lord Jesus Christ*. Whatever activity be ascribed to the believer, the divine initiative is to be discerned throughout, and all is through Jesus Christ our Lord.

10. The manner of our salvation is given in the words *who died for us*, this being the only place in the Thessalonian correspondence where it is said that Christ's death was *for us*. It cannot be inferred from this that Paul was feeling his way to a theology, for at the very time that he wrote this letter he was preaching a gospel where the cross was central (1 Cor. ii. 1ff., xv. 3ff.). Indeed it is difficult to think that he could have alluded to Christ's death in this fashion unless it was already a familiar, non-controversial topic to the Thessalonians. The point is that, in these letters, Paul is occupied primarily with other matters, and accordingly does not deal at length with doctrines which are accepted by all. Lightfoot finds it important that, though Paul's concern is with other matters, he could yet mention this topic. It shows its presence to his mind even when he was busied about other things.

The purpose of His dying for us is our union with Him, and again it is important to notice that this central Pauline concept is present thus early in his ministry. Union with Christ is the entering into a new relationship so enduring in its effects that even death cannot affect it. *Whether we wake or sleep* means 'whether we live or die', both terms referring to physical death and not, as in verse 6 (where the same word is translated *watch* as is here rendered *wake*) being used ethically. The words are a further reassurance for the Thessalonians in their difficulty treated in iv. 13-18. Whichever be our state when He comes again it still follows that we shall live with Him.

11. The section of the Epistle concerned with the second advent is brought to a close with the exhortation to be of good comfort and to build each other up (cf. iv. 18). *Wherefore* means 'on account of the things laid down in the preceding section', all that has been said from iv. 13 onwards being probably in mind. *Comfort* includes the idea of strengthening as well as consoling (see on iii. 2).

The idea of edification is one which Paul uses a good deal. The verb *oikodomeō* is not uncommon in the New Testament in its usual sense of building, as in Mt. vii. 24, 26 of building a house. Jesus used it of building His Church (Mt. xvi. 18), and it is applied to the growth of the Church in Acts ix. 31. But in Paul's hands the verb and the cognate nouns are in frequent use in the sense 'edify', this meaning being found in both his early and his late writings. It perhaps reaches its climax with the thought of believers being built up into a temple of the Holy Spirit (cf. 1 Cor. iii. 9ff.; Eph. ii. 21f.).

The section is rounded off with a tactful *even as also ye do*. Paul is ever anxious to give credit where credit is due. His purpose here is to exhort and encourage the brethren in the right way, not to rebuke them.

VII. GENERAL EXHORTATIONS (v. 12-22)

There are other matters which the apostle feels he must mention to his friends, and as his letter draws to its close he deals with them briefly as they occur to him.

His first point concerns the attitude of the church to its office-bearers. The most probable reading of the situation is that, in the prevailing restlessness, the leaders of the church had rebuked some of the members, possibly those who had been led by their erroneous views concerning the second advent to stop working. Their exhortation had not been given as tactfully as it might have been, nor had it been meekly received. Paul thus addresses the church at large urging members to have a proper respect for their leaders (verses 12, 13), and then, still addressing the church at large, but clearly with the leaders specially in mind, he counsels consideration and patience (verse 14).

12. *We beseech you* is the tone of respectful request. *To know* is used in the full sense of 'to know the worth of', 'to appreciate the value of' (Moffatt 'to respect'). The three following participles are preceded by a common article which indicates that it is one group of persons and not three that is in mind. This means that the people in question are elders, for they alone would exercise the triple function. Frame rejects this idea for 'we are in the period of informal and voluntary leadership'. But elders were appointed from the earliest times (Acts xi. 30, xiv. 23, etc.), and, from the model of the Jewish synagogue, elders are to be expected even in very young churches. It may be possible for an organization to exist without office-bearers of any kind; but it is far from usual, and such evidence as we have does not indicate that the Early Church made the attempt. We do not know the precise function of the elders, and indeed these functions may not have been defined with any exactness. But there seems no reason to doubt that elders were already in existence by the time this letter was written and that the words we are discussing applied to them.

Of the three terms employed, *labour* is quite general, the word properly implying laborious toil (cf. the use of the corresponding noun in i. 3). The function of leadership is implied in the expression *are over you*, the verb (*proistēmi*) being one which can be used of informal leaderships of various kinds. But it is also used of officials, and Moulton-Milligan cite examples from the papyri. Hort thinks it 'morally impossible' that this can be the title of an office, but nevertheless he says,

'It can hardly be doubted that Elders are meant, though no title is given'.[1] With this verb is connected *in the Lord*, which makes it clear that it is spiritual authority that is in mind. It is only as they are *in the Lord* that they are able to exercise effective leadership. The third participle, *admonish*, is found in the New Testament only in the Pauline writings and in a speech of Paul's in Acts xx. 31. It seems to carry a suggestion of blame for wrongdoing (cf. *warn them that are unruly*, verse 14), and so to mean 'admonish' or 'rebuke'.

13. The general sense of this verse is clear enough, although in detail there are difficulties. Thus the verb *esteem* is not found elsewhere in this sense; its usual meaning is simply 'to consider', 'to deem' (as in 2 Thes. iii. 15 where it is rendered *count*). However in this context it does seem to have the meaning given to it by AV. Again, it is not certain whether *in love* should be taken closely with the verb or whether our order should be followed. The difference is between 'hold them in love, and do it exceedingly' (with love the primary idea), and 'esteem them highly' (with 'in love' a somewhat loose addition). On the whole it seems most natural to take the order as in AV. The adverb is a very strong one (see on iii. 10), called by Findlay 'a triple Pauline intensive' meaning 'beyond-exceeding-abundantly' (C.G.T.). The whole sentence then is a strong plea for the leaders to be held in the highest regard. They are to be highly esteemed, not for reasons of personal eminence or office, but *for their work's sake*. They have been spoken of as labouring in the preceding verse, and it is the duty of the rank and file to do all they can to forward the work. Leaders can never do their best work when they are subject to carping criticism from those who should be their followers.

Lightfoot thinks of Paul as gliding off at this point 'from special precepts into a general and comprehensive one'. But it is better to understand behind this next phrase the same situation. From what has gone before it seems clear that the leaders in the Church had not been sufficiently highly re-

[1] *The Christian Ecclesia*, London, 1914, p. 126.

garded, and their authority had been resisted. Also, in all probability, they had not exercised that authority as tactfully as they might have done, and in this situation the injunction *be at peace among yourselves* is very much in place. *Among yourselves* keeps the exhortation general, as applying to all, including the rulers. Had he said 'with them' it would have been a counsel of submission on the part of the rank and file.

14. The counsel given in this verse by the apostle is best interpreted as having special reference to the officers of the church. It should be noticed, however, that it is not specifically addressed to them, but to the church as a whole. In other words, while the officers have a special responsibility with regard to certain duties, these duties are not confined to them, but are, in a measure, the responsibility of all the believers. All should be ready to minister to the needs of the *unruly*, the *feebleminded* and the *weak*.

The first injunction is *warn them that are unruly*. For *warn* see the note on *admonish* in verse 12. *Unruly* is the translation of *ataktous*, a military term signifying the soldier who does not keep in the ranks; from this it comes to mean anything out of place or out of order. Milligan has a long note on this word and its cognates in which he shows that, in the papyri, they are used of being 'idle'. Frame quotes a later letter from Milligan adducing further evidence in support of this conclusion, but he himself thinks it is not so much idleness in general as culpable idleness that is meant. His point is that *ataktous* is a strong word, stronger than the verb used in 1 Cor. vii. 5, 'that ye may give yourselves to fasting and prayer' (i.e. have leisure for fasting and prayer), or that rendered 'idle' in Mt. xx. 3, 6, etc. It denotes culpable idleness or loafing. Such conduct is not to be tolerated in a Christian community.

For *comfort* (*paramutheomai*) see note on ii. 11. *Feebleminded* does not seem a good rendering of *oligopsuchous*, which means rather 'faint-hearted'. It may refer to those who naturally lack courage, or to those who have become discouraged by reason of particular circumstances; for example, those who had grown despondent because their friends had died before the second advent (see iv. 13ff.). *Support the weak* must refer to the weak spiritually, not physically (cf. the treatment of the weak in Rom. xiv; 1 Cor. viii). The verb *antechesthe* is used in the New Testament of holding on to something, cleaving to a person (cf. Lk. xvi. 13). The weak need to feel that they are not alone. Accordingly the strong should 'hold to them' and in this way give them the support that they require.

Following the injunctions for particular classes we have one for *all* men. The verb *makrothumeō*, 'to be patient', is the opposite of *oxuthumeō*, 'to be short-tempered', and it gives the idea of a steady patience. It is easy to lose patience with one's fellows for various reasons, good as well as bad, but for the Christian longsuffering is to be the rule.

15. There is now a change from the second to the third person, 'see you that no-one render . . . '. It is not only that each man is to take heed to his own conduct; the whole community has a responsibility for the individuals comprising it. This is again a charge which has special application to the office-bearers; but it is not without its relevance to all. Every Christian should be giving his attention to the conduct of the whole group.

This prohibition of retaliation is found also in Rom. xii. 17 and 1 Pet. iii. 9, with the same Greek verb and the same expression *evil for evil*. It is possible that it goes back to some saying of the Lord (the same duty is inculcated in Mt. v. 43f.). Faced with opposition from both Jews and Gentiles, and with some differences within the church itself, this must have been exceedingly difficult for the Thessalonians, yet Paul does not hesitate to put the matter plainly to them. Christian teaching is not meant to be applied only when circumstances are easy. Christianity is a robust faith, empowered with a divine dynamic, and is to be lived out even under the most trying circumstances.

The negative injunction is followed by the positive *ever follow that which is good*. In this context *good* stands over against *evil* in the previous clause, and so denotes, primarily, what is helpful to others, rather than the pursuit of the moral ideal. It is the attitude of returning blessing for cursing, of being actively friendly in the face of hostility. This is not to be understood of isolated small acts of kindness, but of a life lived in an attitude of Christian love, as the *ever*, and the continuous present *follow* show. It is also a duty which Christian men should exercise both among themselves, and also toward all men, whether they are believers or not. Christian charity is not to be circumscribed or restricted, but freely extended wherever there is the need.

16. The injunction to *Rejoice evermore* is at first sight a little surprising coming from one who had had to suffer as much and as continually as had Paul. But he had learned that affliction and deep joy may go together (2 Cor. vi. 10), and could rejoice in tribulations (Rom. v. 3; cf. Acts xvi. 25). So he can counsel perpetual rejoicing even to a church which was suffering so greatly. It is of interest that in his other letter to a Macedonian church, that to the Philippians, the note of joy is likewise often struck. Few things about the New Testament are more remarkable than this continual stress on joy. Our information about the Early Church indicates that, from an outward point of view, there was little that could cause rejoicing. But they were 'in Christ,' and because they were in Him they had learned the truth of His words 'your joy no man taketh from you' (Jn. xvi. 22). So it is that the various derivatives of joy occur with startling frequency throughout the New Testament. The word for 'grace', for example, and one of the verbs meaning 'to forgive' are from this root. New Testament Christianity is permeated with the spirit of holy joy, and there is no reason why twentieth century Christianity should not have the same joyfulness.

17. 'It is not in the moving of the lips, but in the elevation of the heart to God, that the essence of prayer consists' (Lightfoot), and it is this which enables us to carry into practice the injunction *Pray without ceasing*. It is not possible for us to spend all our time with the words of prayer on our lips, but it is possible for us to be all our days in the spirit of prayer, realizing our dependence on God for all that we have and are, realizing something of His presence with us wherever we may be, and yielding ourselves continually to Him for the doing of His will. Where there is such an inward state it will find outward expression in verbal prayer, and in this connection we should notice the frequent ejaculatory prayers throughout Paul's letters. Prayer was so natural and so continual with the great apostle that it found its way inevitably into his correspondence.

18. Paul had learned that, even in difficulties and tribulations, God is teaching us valuable lessons, and that, accordingly, such trials are to be welcomed and used (cf. Rom. v. 3ff.). Arising out of this recognition of the divine sovereignty and providence is the importance of giving thanks under all circumstances. It is often difficult to see the brighter side of a particular trial; but if it is our deep conviction that God is over all, and that His hand is in the particular tribulation we are undergoing, then we cannot but recognize His goodness and make our act of thanksgiving. *In every thing* is not quite the same as 'at every time' (the two are differentiated in 2 Cor. ix. 8) and means 'in every circumstance'.

For this is the will of God . . . almost certainly refers to all three injunctions, even though *this* is singular. The point is that they form a unity, and are bracketed together. *Will* has no article, for it is not the totality of the divine will that is being spoken of. There are other things that God would have us do, but these three are part of His will for us. The addition *in Christ Jesus* is characteristically Pauline. The will is made known in Christ, and it is in Christ that men are given the dynamic that enables them to carry out that divine will.

19. The verb *quench* signifies the putting out of a fire (Mk. ix. 48, etc.), and is an appropriate word to use of the Spirit, whose coming was with 'tongues, like as of fire' (Acts ii. 3), and who brings warmth and light to the Christian life. The use of the Greek negative *mē* with the present imperative here denotes a command to cease from doing something already in process, and not simply a warning to avoid this kind of thing in the future.

Most commentators take the injunction as referring to ecstatic gifts of the Spirit, such as speaking with tongues, and understand the verse to mean that some of the more conservative church members were frowning on the enthusiasts with their eager pursuit of the more spectacular gifts of the Spirit. In Corinthians Paul was to have occasion to curb an exaggerated dependence on this kind of thing; but here, it is said, there is the reverse situation. It is possible that this is what is in Paul's mind, for an injunction to cease from quenching the Spirit is unusual. But the evidence cited cannot be said to be strong, and the words are very general. In Eph. iv. 30 there is a similar general statement, the verb being 'grieve', and most would agree that there is no reference in that passage to the ecstatic gifts. It is possible to quench the Spirit (or to grieve Him) by such matters as those mentioned earlier in the Epistle—for example despondency, idleness, immorality and the like—and it is best to take the word in such a general sense.

20. One particular manifestation of the Spirit's activity is singled out for special mention, *Despise not prophesyings* (cf. 1 Cor. xiv. 1). As was the case among the Corinthians, some of the Thessalonians may have thought more of spectacular gifts, such as the gift of tongues, than of prophecy (see 1 Cor. xiv), and Paul may be seeking to redress the balance. But there is no evidence. A more likely conjecture is that there had been prophetic outbursts in connection with second advent expectations. At all times in history the two have tended to go together, and at all times one result has been that those who are not caught up with the advent speculation tend to regard prophecy lightly. There are indications in this Epistle that some of the members had been over-enthusiastic in their advent views, and that there were others who had rather tactlessly rebuked them (see notes on verses 12ff.). There is nothing improbable in the idea that, in the process, they had come to look slightingly on prophecy.

The New Testament clearly regards the prophets as being important. They were, in fact, so highly regarded that they were classed with apostles (Eph. ii. 20, iii. 5) and, more formally, ranked as second to the apostles (1 Cor. xii. 28; Eph. iv. 11). Prophecy is several times referred to as the gift of God (1 Cor. xii. 28; Eph. iv. 11), or of the Spirit (1 Cor. xii. 10). Commentators in recent years have been at pains to point out that prophets were forth-tellers rather than fore-tellers, and this is supported by the fact that their characteristic function seems to have been exhortation (see Acts xv. 32, and also the notable discussion in 1 Cor. xiv). Essentially the prophet was a man who could say 'Thus saith the Lord'. But it should not be overlooked that this might, and sometimes did, include the foretelling of the future (Acts xi. 27f., xxi. 10f.).

21. Paul, however, is not advocating an uncritical acceptance of anything uttered by a man who claims to be a prophet, so he immediately proceeds *Prove all things*. This is a general precept, and is not to be limited to the testing of spiritual gifts (cf. Moffatt, 'test them all'), though it has its application to that problem and thus is very much in place here. The verb *dokimazō* (*prove*) is often used of testing metals, and may derive from this practice. It comes to mean testing in general, and acquires the secondary meaning of approving as a result of test. Here the meaning is plainly 'test', and the idea is 'avoid gullibility', 'apply spiritual tests to all that claims to be from God'.

These words are connected by most of the early Greek commentators with a saying attributed to Jesus, 'Be approved bankers' (or 'moneychangers', i.e. testers of coin. See the passages in Lightfoot). If this is a genuine saying of our Lord, and the evidence makes this likely, it may have been in Paul's mind as he wrote these words. At any rate the same kind of attitude is being inculcated. M. R. James thinks these words of Paul 'are really a comment on the saying, and show its meaning'.[1]

[1] *The Apocryphal New Testament*, Oxford, 1926, p. 35.

But it is not enough to apply the test: that which the test approves must be held fast. There are two Greek words in common use for *good, kalos* and *agathos.* While they are very closely allied in meaning the distinction appears to be that the former, which is the one employed here, signifies that which is good itself, while the other denotes that which is good in its effects (it is used, for example, in verse 15). The present word is sometimes used of coins which ring true, that is of genuine as compared with counterfeit coin. It is very much to the point in this context.

22. The positive injunction is followed by the negative. The form employed is a strong one with the preposition *apo* (as in iv. 3) used to emphasize the complete separation of the believer from evil. There is some doubt as to the meaning of the word *eidous* rendered *appearance,* and again, whether *evil* is to be regarded as a noun, as in AV, or as an adjective. Not much depends on the latter point, for in either case the meaning is the same (as Calvin pointed out). The word *eidos* means the outward appearance or form (Lk. iii. 22, 'shape'), without any notion of unreality. It is also used in the sense 'sort, species, kind'. AV takes it in a third sense, 'semblance' as opposed to reality, but this does not seem to be attested elsewhere, and it is unlikely that the apostle would be concerned only with outward appearance (there is no word 'even' here to give the meaning, 'even from the appearance of evil'). Our choice seems to be between 'every visible form of evil' (with no notion of unreality), and 'every kind of evil'. The use of the word elsewhere in the New Testament favours the former; but there are enough examples of the term meaning 'kind' in the papyri to make the second quite possible. And in view of the context I am inclined to accept it. Paul is urging his friends to eschew evil of every kind.

The change from *that which is good* (lit. 'the good') in the previous verse to 'every kind of evil' in this is significant. The good is one, but evil is manifold, and is to be avoided in all its forms.

VIII. CONCLUSION (v. 23-28)

23. The conjunction *de* really has an adversative force, 'but'. Paul has been exhorting the Thessalonians to a course of conduct which is impossible in man's own strength, and he utters a prayer which reminds them of the source of the power which alone would enable them to live in this way. God is spoken of as *the God of peace*, a designation Paul often employs in such prayers and aspirations towards the end of his letters (cf. 2 Thes. iii. 16; Rom. xv. 33, xvi. 20; 2 Cor. xiii. 11; Phil. iv. 9). *Peace* (see note on i. 1) is spiritual prosperity in the widest sense, and so characteristic is it of God to bestow this gift that He may be spoken of as *the God of peace*.

The prayer is that God may *sanctify you wholly*. There is a manward aspect of sanctification in that we are called upon to yield up our wills for the doing of God's will. But the power manifest in the sanctified life is not human, but divine, and Paul's prayer is phrased in the light of this. In the deepest sense our sanctification is the work of God within us. This work of sanctification may be ascribed to the Son (Eph. v. 26) or to the Spirit (Rom. xv. 16), but in any case it is divine. The word *wholly* is an unusual one (*holoteleis*), being found only here in the New Testament. It is a combination of the ideas of wholeness and completion, and Lightfoot suggests that the meaning may be given here as 'may He sanctify you so that ye be entire'.

The second part of Paul's prayer runs 'may your whole spirit and soul and body be preserved blameless' (rather than 'I pray God . . .'). This is sometimes used as an argument for a trichotomous view of man, as against a dichotomous view, but this is probably unjustified. Paul is not here concerned to give a theoretical analysis of the nature of man, but is uttering a fervent prayer that the entire man may be preserved. Milligan thinks that the threefold petition is meant for 'man's whole being, whether on its immortal, its personal, or its bodily side'.

That the unity of man is being emphasized is indicated by the fact that both the verb and the adjective *whole* are singular, although they apply to all three. The word *whole* is from a different root from that of the adverb *wholly*, and it denotes 'complete in all its parts'. It is used in the LXX of Dt. xxvii. 6 of stones for the altar, and writers like Philo and Josephus use it of sacrificial victims. It is therefore possible that Paul has in mind the presentation of the whole man as a living sacrifice (cf. Rom. xii. 1). The prayer is that the whole man be *preserved blameless*, a word being used which is found only here in the New Testament. It is interesting to notice that it is found also in the inscriptions on some tombs found at Thessalonica.

It is characteristic of these Epistles, with their interest in the second coming, that the prayer concludes with a reference to this great event. AV is misleading in its rendering *unto the coming*, for the preposition is *en* not *eis*, and the meaning is 'at the coming'. The prayer is not that they may be kept until the coming, but that, at the coming, they may be preserved; i.e. there is in mind the thought of the judgment with all that that implies.

24. The faithfulness of God is the ground for certainty that the prayer offered will be answered. Chrysostom gives the meaning in these words, 'This happens not from my prayers, he says, but from the purpose with which he called you' (cited in Frame). The faithfulness of God is often dwelt upon in the New Testament, as in 2 Thes. iii. 3; 1 Cor. i. 9, x. 13; 2 Cor. i. 18; 2 Tim. ii. 13; Heb. x. 23, xi. 11.

God is spoken of as *he that calleth you* (present participle), not 'he that called you', and we have the thought of God in His capacity as Caller, the participle being timeless. This is followed by an unusual use of the verb *do*: it is used absolutely (there is no *it* in the Greek). The effect of this is to emphasize the doing, to fasten attention on the fact that God will bring to pass what He has begun. This is strengthened by the *also*. The faithful Caller will *also* act.

25. We catch a glimpse of a very human Paul in this simple request for prayer. Although he was a man of great gifts and of undoubted eminence in the Church, he yet felt himself to be dependent on the prayers of his friends. Notice the affectionate address, *brethren*. For similar requests for prayer see 2 Thes.

iii. 1f. (where the request is particularized); Rom. xv. 30; Eph. vi. 19; Col. iv. 3f.; Heb. xiii. 18, and cf. Phil. i. 19.

26. 'In the ancient world one kissed the hand, breast, knee, or foot of a superior, and the cheek of a friend. Herodotus (1, 134) mentions kissing the lips as a custom of the Persians. Possibly from them it came to the Jews'.[1] Not a great deal is known of kissing in the Early Church, but it is usually held that men kissed men, and women women, and that the kiss was on the cheek. There does not seem to be any connection with liturgical practices; but the kiss would naturally be exchanged on the Lord's day when the brethren came together, and thus it is not surprising that in later days it came to be included in the services of the Church, notably the service of Holy Communion (though not confined to this). In time it became the custom for the kiss to be exchanged between men and women, and Clement of Alexandria objected to 'resounding kisses in Church which made suspicious and evil reports among the heathen' (cited in Neil). Abuses of this kind led to its restriction, and there are several regulations dealing with it in the early Church Councils.

Here the meaning is 'Give all the brethren a kiss from me' (cf. 'My love be with you all', 1 Cor. xvi. 24). It is Paul's warm greeting to his friends in the Thessalonian church. There are references to such a 'holy kiss' in Rom. xvi. 16; 1 Cor. xvi. 20; 2 Cor. xiii. 12, and to a 'kiss of love' in 1 Pet. v. 14.

Much is sometimes made of the fact that Paul says *Greet all the brethren*, and not simply 'Greet one another' (see *Introduction*, p. 26). But probably no great stress should be laid on the *all*, which is not in a specially emphatic position. If this is Paul's greeting to the church, and not an injunction as to what their mode of greeting each other should be, then it is natural enough for him to refer to *all the brethren*.

27. The strength of the language here is surprising. *I charge you by the Lord* means 'I put you on your oath as Chris-

[1]Toy on Proverbs xxiv. 26.

tians', the verb being *enorkizō*. This rare verb is apparently a strengthened form of *horkizō* (Mk. v. 7; Acts xix. 13), where we might have anticipated something like 'See that this letter is read to all'. There may also be significance in the fact that he says 'I', not 'we', although the emphatic *ego* is not employed.

The explanation of this is not easy. Some see in it a reference to a divided church, such that some of the members would not wish to have the letter read to all, or perhaps that some would not want to hear it. There may be something in this; but, while there are indications of certain tensions within the church, as we have noted in the exposition, yet there is nothing to indicate that the church was as seriously divided as all that. We cannot imagine Paul praising the church so highly if this were the case. It is much the same with the suggestion that this is one of the earliest Epistles, and the custom of reading it to all the brethren was not yet established. If this were all, there seems no need of 'I adjure'! Lightfoot suggests that Paul may have had a presentiment 'that a wrong use might be made of his name and authority. Such a suspicion was entirely justified by subsequent occurrences (2 Thes. ii. 2)'. This may be so, although it is dangerous to appeal to possible presentiments for our explanation of difficulties.

The best explanation is probably to be found in the intense desire of Paul and the Thessalonians to see each other again, and the impossibility of that occurring in the prevailing circumstances. Paul was most anxious to avoid giving the wrong impression, and thus uses strong words to make sure that his message comes before everybody, and is plainly seen to be intended to come before everybody. It is possible also that he has a special concern for those who had been bereaved, and who might perhaps be absent when the letter was read. He makes it certain that they will not miss the comfort he is sending them.

The word *read* (*anagnōsthenai*) is found in the sense of reading aloud, and also simply of reading. Some maintain that reading was always aloud in antiquity, but Lake and Cadbury maintain that it is 'surely incredible that educated Greeks and Romans had not learned to read silently'.[1] Milligan cites examples of the use of the word in the sense of reading as well as of reading aloud. Here it is clearly reading aloud that is meant. Reading during public worship is not implied, though in time this became usual, and Paul's letters became accepted as sacred Scripture.

Holy brethren is an unusual phrase, found nowhere else (though we do find *holy apostles*, Eph. iii. 5). As the adjective seems redundant (the brethren were by definition *holy*), is lacking in the better manuscripts, and could easily have crept into the text from the previous verse, it seems better to omit it.

28. In place of the customary 'Farewell' (*erōros, errōsthe*) Paul always has a prayer for grace for his readers as the conclusion to his letters. Our present verse may be taken as the typical form which was sometimes expanded (as in the Trinitarian form in 2 Cor. xiii. 14) and sometimes shortened (Col. iv. 18; and so in the Pastorals). The concluding portion was written by the apostle himself (the main body of the letter having been penned by an amanuensis) as we see from 2 Thes. iii. 17. The precise point at which he took the pen seems to have varied a little (cf. Gal. vi. 11), and it is likely, from the first person singular, that in this letter it was before verse 27 at any rate.

Amen is not a characteristic ending, and it is omitted here by the better manuscripts.

The subscription, 'The first epistle unto the Thessalonians was written from Athens', does not occur in the oldest manuscripts, and is almost certainly a scribal gloss. The late manuscripts which contain these words differ in important particulars, some for example reading only 'The first epistle unto the Thessalonians', while one has 'Corinth' in place of 'Athens'. It seems clear enough that the various readings are simply so many attempts to read the evidence and not the result of reliable traditions. Little weight is to be attached to them.

[1] On Acts viii. 30.

II THESSALONIANS: ANALYSIS

II THESSALONIANS: COMMENTARY

I. GREETING (i. 1, 2)

1, 2. The address is exactly the same as in the first Epistle, except that *our* is included with *Father*, making it clear that it is God as Father of believers that is in mind, rather than as Father of the Lord Jesus Christ. The greeting is also the same as that in the first Epistle, with the addition of the words which follow *peace* in verse 2. These words are probably absent from the first letter, but they are genuine here. This form of greeting is usual in Paul's Epistles, being found in each one with the exception of 1 Thessalonians (though the words *and the Lord Jesus Christ* are lacking in Colossians in the better manuscripts). It reminds us that the source of the Christian's *grace and peace* is in no less a One than God. Paul often associates *grace* with Christ, and *peace* with the Father, but in his greetings he prefers to make no distinction.

II. PRAYER (i. 3–12)

(a) Thanksgiving (i. 3–5)

3. As in the first Epistle Paul begins with thanksgiving for the Christian graces evident in the Thessalonians. He had used some flattering expressions about them in that letter, and it is likely that, in their subsequent communication with him, they had modestly disclaimed being worthy of such praise. Thus Paul insists that his praise was quite in order: *We are bound to thank God always for you.* Some have seen in this a rather stiff and formal approach, quite different from that in the first Epistle, but this seems to be discounted by the warm expressions which follow. The Greek word *opheilomen* (*we are bound*) conveys the idea of personal obligation (*dei*, which is often used in similar contexts, would rather signify a compulsion arising out of external circumstances). *As it is meet* is not simply a repetition of the same thought, but means 'It is no more than you deserve'.

113

Paul is insistent that the merits of the Thessalonians are real, and this imposes on him an obligation to recognize the fact.

The points for which he gives thanks are two, the growth of their faith, and the abundance of their love. It is interesting that in I Thes. iii. 10 Paul had shown himself anxious about what was lacking in their faith; but now, a short time after, he is able to give thanks for the vigorous growth of that faith. He uses a compound verb, *huperauxanei*, which gives the idea of a 'growing beyond'.

In I Thes. iii. 12 he had prayed that God would make them 'to increase and abound in love one toward another, and toward all men'; now he is able to give thanks to God for the answer to that prayer. *Charity* would be better translated 'love', for the Greek is *agapē* (as in I Thes. iii. 12). *Aboundeth, pleonazei*, differs from *groweth exceedingly*, in that the latter is a word applying strictly to organic growth (like the growth of a healthy plant), while the former denotes a wide dispersal. This love is being exercised by the entire community (*of you all*), and is also being shown by each individual (*every one of you*). Though Paul has some salutary rebukes to administer before the letter is finished, yet he is glad to begin by paying a tribute to the Christian love which permeated the community. No one is excluded.

In the first Epistle he had given thanks for their *patience of hope*, as well as for their faith and love, but the omission here is not significant, for he uses the same word *patience* in the next verse as one of the things about which he boasts.

4. The result (*hōste*, 'so that', indicates consequence) of the increase of faith and love was that Paul and his companions boasted of the Thessalonians to other Christians. Those who maintain that the tone of this Epistle is colder than that of the preceding naturally find the emphatic expressions used here a little difficult to explain. *We ourselves* (Gk. *autous hēmas*) is unusually strong in such a connection, and draws attention to the boasters, and the verb translated *glory* is the compound *enkauchasthai*, not the simple verb which Paul generally employs.

The meaning appears to be that the habit of the preachers was not to boast of their converts (in 1 Thes. i. 9 it is other people who boast to Paul, not he to them); but in this case the merits are so outstanding that even the founders of the church are constrained to sing its praises.

Matter for this boasting is the converts' *patience* (see note on 1 Thes. i. 3) and *faith* in their troubles. *Faith* here is understood by some to mean 'faithfulness', 'fidelity', because of the connection with *patience*; but the reason does not seem adequate. The Greek *pistis* can denote 'fidelity', but in the New Testament it nearly always means 'faith' (see note on iii. 2). In the previous verse it has been used in this usual sense, and there seems no reason for understanding it differently here. Amid their difficulties they had preserved a trust in God (cf. note on 1 Thes. iii. 5).

Tribulations (*thlipsesin*) is a more general word than *persecutions* (*diōgmois*). Whereas the latter denotes the assaults made on the Christians on account of their Christian profession, the former stands in general for any trials and troubles they might meet, whether in the course of the persecution or in any other way. The use of the present tense, *ye endure*, indicates that the troubles were not a matter of past history, but were continuing at the moment of writing.

5. The difficulty here is that the *persecutions and tribulations* which the Thessalonians had been enduring seem, on the face of it, to deny rather than to prove *the righteous judgment of God*. But probably we should understand the *manifest token* not as referring to the difficulties of the Christians (as Rutherford's translation, 'And indeed these sufferings attest the equity of God'), but to the whole of the preceding clause. It is not the persecutions, but the attitude of the Thessalonians in the persecutions which is the decisive thing. Not suffering as such, but the attitude of faith in the midst of suffering inflicted for the kingdom's sake (*for which ye also suffer*) is cited as the proof. Such constancy and faith could come only from the action of God within them; and if God has so inspired them there is clear evidence that He does not intend them to fall short of the final attainment of the kingdom (cf. Phil. i. 28).

Lightfoot understands *the righteous judgment* (which in this form occurs only here in Paul, though Rom. ii. 5 is similar) in terms of 'the law of compensation by which the sufferers of this world shall rest hereafter and the persecutors of this world shall suffer hereafter'. While this thought is much in mind (cf. the next verse) the idea here is bigger. It is part of God's *righteous judgment* to use tribulations to bring His own people to perfection.

This seems to be involved in the Greek construction which follows (*eis to* with the infinitive) which emphasizes the idea of purpose. The judgment was with a view to their being counted worthy of the kingdom. The verb *kataxioō* means not 'to make worthy', or 'to be worthy', but 'to declare worthy' or 'to count worthy', reminding us strongly of that other great Pauline word *dikaioō*, 'to justify', in the sense of 'to declare' or 'count as just'. By his choice of this word the apostle is excluding human merit even in a section where he is drawing attention to a noteworthy piece of endurance, and is emphasizing that attainment to the kingdom is not the result of human endeavour at all, but of the grace of God. (For the *kingdom of God* see note on 1 Thes. ii. 12.)

For which (huper) ye also suffer does not mean 'in order to gain which', but 'on behalf of which', 'in the interests of which'. It is precisely the disinterested nature of their sufferings which afforded the evidence that God was in them.

(b) Divine judgment (i. 6–10)

6. These statements regarding God's purpose are, in effect, a deduction from the general principle which Paul now proceeds to lay down. It is cast in a hypothetical form (*seeing* is our rendering of the Greek *eiper* 'if indeed'). This must not be held to cast doubt on the proposition; it is rather a rhetorical understatement, which we find used of things so far beyond doubt as the indwelling of the Holy Spirit in the believer (Rom. viii. 9), or the existence of idols (1 Cor. viii. 5). So sure is Paul here that what he is saying is universally admitted that he can afford to cast it into this hypothetical form. If (as all admit) it is a righteous thing with God, then consequences follow.

Some have found in the words of this verse such an expression of the *lex talionis* that they feel it cannot be Christian, and the hypothesis of a Jewish interpolator has even been produced. But such a position cannot be sustained. If the universe is a moral universe we cannot think of sin as going unpunished. The sinner always hopes that he will escape any penalty for his sin; but because God is over all, this is utterly impossible. 'Punishment is the other half of sin', said James Denney, a truth to which this verse gives emphatic expression, grounding it, as is meet, not in general philosophical opinions, but in the righteous nature of God. For *recompense* see note on 1 Thes. iii. 9 and for *tribulation* on 1 Thes. i. 6.

7. The positive side of the retribution now succeeds the negative, and Paul thinks of *rest* (*anesin*) for the *troubled*. The word has the idea of relief from tension (originally it signified the slackening of a taut bow string). It is only once used in the New Testament outside the Pauline writings, and in Paul it is usually opposed to the word rendered *tribulation* in the preceding verse. So Paul points his friends forward to the prospect of release from the afflictions that tormented them. Sometimes it is suggested that this is an unworthy motive, but such suggestions usually emanate from the comfortable. It is a matter of history that those who are passing through suffering for the Lord's sake do not, as a rule, despise the prospect of final blessedness. This is not the whole of the gospel, but it is an authentic part of it, and we are not wise to overlook it. *With us* is a reminder that Paul and his companions were likewise subject to persecution. It is 'a sigh on his own account' (Findlay, C.G.T.).

From this point to the end of verse 10 the structure is so markedly rhythmical that a number of scholars have felt that Paul is quoting from some Jewish Psalm. Way calls it 'The

Hymn of the Second Coming'. It may be that Paul is quoting, but there seems no real reason for denying the passage to him.

The first point is the coming of the Lord Jesus. The Greek literally means 'in the revelation of the Lord Jesus', which is not quite the same as AV, *when the Lord Jesus shall be revealed.* It is not only that the retribution will take place when Christ is revealed: the retribution itself is part of the revelation. There are various words used in the New Testament to denote the final consummation. We have already had *parousia* in 1 Thes. iii. 13, etc. Here *apokalupsis* presents it in the aspect of an uncovering or unfolding. It is the revelation of a Person at present concealed from the world. He is to be revealed 'with the angels of his power'. AV *mighty angels* takes the genitive as a Semitism, equivalent to an adjective. This is possible; but it seems more in accordance with the thought of the passage to take the literal translation. It is not the power of the angels that is being stressed, but that of the Lord.

8. *In flaming fire* should probably be taken with the preceding rather than the following, though either is grammatically possible. But the meaning appears to be that the *flaming fire* is the robe of the returning Lord (cf. Ex. iii. 2; Is. lxvi. 15; Rev. i. 13ff.), so awe-ful and so majestic will be His appearance.

From His appearance we turn to His activity. *Taking vengeance* is really 'giving vengeance' the expression being Hebraistic. In the Old Testament vengeance is the prerogative of Jehovah alone (see Dt. xxxii. 35), and the fact that it is here ascribed to the Lord Jesus is unmistakable evidence that He was regarded as, in the fullest sense, divine.

The Greek has separate articles with the two expressions *them that know not God* and (them) *that obey not the gospel.* The most natural way of understanding this is to take it as signifying two distinct groups of people. Some, indeed, have distinguished between them so thoroughly that they see the Gentiles in the former expression and the Jews in the latter (cf. Way's translation 'on those heathen who know not God, on those Jews who refuse obedience. . . .'). This, however, seems to be reading too much into the passage. Rather, *them that know not God* is a way of designating, not the heathen, but those, whoever they may be, who are guilty of culpable neglect of such knowledge of God as He has been pleased to vouchsafe to them. What is in mind is rejection of the proffered light (as in 1 Thes. iv. 5). Them *that obey not the gospel*, therefore, is a more specific example of the foregoing, and refers to the rejection of the ultimate revelation of God's saving activity. It must be borne in mind, too, that this whole passage is deeply tinged with Hebraistic modes of thought and, in the manner of many Old Testament passages, the second expression may be simply taking up and filling out the thought of the first.

9. The relative pronoun used is the relative of quality (*hoitines*), 'who are of such a kind as to', and draws attention to the fitness of these men for the punishment they will meet. *Shall be punished* is literally 'shall pay penalty', the last word (*dikē*) being from the same root as 'righteous' (*dikaios*). The thought of the verse is not of an unreasoning infliction of vindictive punishment, but of the meting out of merited desert. The penalty is given in some detail. *Destruction* is not to be understood in the sense of 'annihilation', but of complete ruin. It is the loss of all that makes life worth living. Coupled with the adjective *eternal* it is the opposite of eternal life. The exact expression occurs again in 4 Macc. x. 15 (and there only in the Greek Bible), where it is the lot of the wicked tyrant, and is set over against 'the happy death' of the martyr. It is exclusion from the *presence* (literally 'face') of God in accordance with the typical Scriptural position that the real sting of sin is that it separates from fellowship with the Lord. *The glory of his power* points us to another aspect of the same thing, for *glory* means something like 'the visible manifestation of the greatness of God'. Notice the almost incidental, but very telling, reference to His strength. The Thessalonians were feeling the power of other men, but Paul reminds them that there is One mightier. (For the expressions used here cf. Is. ii. 10, 19, 21.)

These are solemn words and the utter finality of the lot of

the wicked is clear. As Denney says, 'If there is any truth in Scripture at all, this is true—that those who stubbornly refuse to submit to the gospel, and to love and obey Jesus Christ, incur at the Last Advent an infinite and irreparable loss. They pass into a night on which no morning dawns.'

10. The *when* which introduces this verse is the indefinite *hotan* indicating that the time of the coming is not known. But whenever it takes place its distinguishing characteristic will be its glory. Paul introduces here the interesting thought that this glory will be seen *in his saints*. The verb is a compound meaning 'be glorified-in' and it is followed by another 'in' emphasizing that the saints will be, as it were, a mirror reflecting something of the greatness of the glory of their Lord (cf. 1 Jn. iii. 2, 'when he shall appear, we shall be like him').

To be admired is an example of the use of 'admire' in a sense no longer familiar (cf. Rev. xvii. 6), namely, 'to be wondered at' (Phillips: 'It will be a breath-taking wonder'). The idea is that the glory of that day will far surpass anything of which we can have any idea before we behold it, and when we do behold it we shall be lost in amazement.

The aorist participle in *in all them that believe* has sometimes caused strange interpretations (e.g. that noted by Lightfoot, 'the past tense is used here to denote that faith would then have been absorbed in sight and ceased to be'). The initial step of faith is the decisive step, and believing may thus be taken as synonymous with becoming a Christian. But this act may be regarded in various ways. The present may be used to emphasize the continuing nature of faith. Or the aorist may draw attention to the decisive character of the act of making one's decision for Christ. The perfect combines the two and stresses the permanence of the result. Here, then, the use of the aorist indicates those who have taken the decisive step of faith.

The construction in the parenthesis *because our testimony among you was believed* is very awkward, and this has led to a variety of interpretations. Hort found it so difficult that he

resorted to the extreme step of making a conjectural emendation
(*epistōthē*, 'was confirmed', for *episteuthē*, 'was believed'), this
being one of the very few occasions when he adopted this
procedure. It is impossible to go into all the difficulties here,
but Lightfoot's suggestion that the passage is elliptical seems
best, the meaning then being '. . . in all them that believed,
and *therefore in you*, for our testimony was believed by you'.
The testimony borne among the Thessalonians had produced
the desired fruit.

(c) The content of Paul's prayer (i. 11, 12)

11. *Wherefore* is really 'to this end' (*eis ho*), and probably refers
to the whole of the preceding section. Paul's prayer for them
grows out of his thanksgiving for them and his contemplation
of the blessed things to come. The prayer is that the Thessalonians may grow in things spiritual; it is expressed in a
number of different ways. First, *count you worthy*. It is probably
not true that Paul is here contemplating the possibility of his
converts' falling away from the faith. His attention is fixed on
the glory that is to be revealed, and he prays that on the last
day they may be counted worthy of having been called, i.e.,
that during the intervening time they may live in such a
manner as to ensure this commendation. The term *calling*
(*klēsis*) is usually applied to the initial act whereby God calls
men to be His own, and this is probably in view here. But it is
also likely that Paul is thinking of the final consummation of
that calling. He speaks of *our God*, uniting his converts with
himself in contemplating their common Master.

AV inserts *his* before *goodness* and thus makes the next
petition refer to God's good pleasure and God's goodness.
Against this, however, is the fact that this word for *goodness*
(*agathōsunē*) is never used of God elsewhere in the New Testament. The parallel expression *and the work of faith with power*
seems much more naturally to refer to the faith exercised by the
believers. Milligan adds the point that it would be more
natural to have the article before *eudokia* if it referred to God.
These considerations make it likely that *his* should be omitted

(there is nothing corresponding to it in the Greek) and *the good pleasure* and the *goodness* be taken to refer to the Thessalonians. The source is thought of as being in God, for he prays that He may *fulfil* these things. Paul is praying, then, that God would bring about within the Thessalonians the goodness of will (*eudokia* means 'good resolve' and not merely 'good desire') which leads to goodness of action. It is like the collect for Easter Day, 'We humbly beseech thee, that as by thy special grace preventing us thou dost put into our minds good desires, so by thy continual help we may bring the same to good effect', as more than one commentator has pointed out.

Coupled with this is the *work of faith* (see note on 1 Thes. i. 3). Paul never thinks of faith as a passive thing, but as something which is ceaselessly active appropriating God's blessings and using God's power for God's service. The addition *with power* is to be taken with both clauses. Paul prays that the power of God may be seen both in the good pleasure of goodness, and in the work of faith. Neither is to be done in merely human strength.

12. *That the name of our Lord Jesus Christ may be glorified in you.* The 'name' in Biblical times stood for the whole personality and was an expression of the personality. To 'glorify the name' was to exalt a person. In this further petition, therefore, Paul looks for the Thessalonians so to produce the qualities of Christian character which have just been mentioned that the effect would be to exalt the Saviour who had produced such works of mighty power within them. Some see in the glorification of the name of Christ a reference to the glories of the second advent. But while the Parousia is not out of mind throughout this whole section, the primary emphasis here would seem to be on the quality of life produced in the Thessalonians by the indwelling Christ. The being *glorified in you, and ye in him* reminds us of the words of our Lord in Jn. xvii. 1, 10, 21ff. They are not to be glorified 'with' Him, but 'in' Him, as He was to be in them. The closest of unions is in mind.

All this is *according to the grace of our God.* As in the previous verse everything is ascribed to its basic cause in God. It is not in the power of the Thessalonians to bring glory to the name of the Lord. *Grace* in the New Testament is a singularly rich word, and here lacks none of its force. The ideas especially emphasized are those of the favour shown by God to the unworthy, and made available for them through the work of Christ, and of the gifts He bestows upon men. The purpose of such gifts of inner strength in the Holy Spirit is that men may live the life envisaged in the earlier part of this verse.

It is grammatically possible to understand *our God* as synonymous with the following *Lord Jesus Christ* since there is one article. But *Kurios* (*Lord*) often occurs without the article, like a proper name. This is probably the case here, so that we should understand the expression as referring to both the Father and the Son (as in AV).

III. THE PAROUSIA (ii. 1–12)

(a) The day of the Lord not yet present (ii. 1, 2)

As in the first Epistle the main part of the letter begins in the second chapter at the conclusion of the introductory prayer. It concerns erroneous ideas about the second coming which some of the converts had enthusiastically espoused. In writing thus Paul is supplementing what he had already told them by word of mouth (see verse 5). It is unfortunate for us that we have no means of knowing what he had already said to them, for what he writes is full of allusions to his oral teaching. The result is that this passage is probably the most obscure and difficult in the whole of the Pauline correspondence and the many gaps in our knowledge have given rise to the most extravagant speculations. It will be well for us to bear in mind that we do not possess the key to everything that is here said, and accordingly to maintain some reserve in our interpretations.[1]

1. Paul introduces the section with the language of entreaty as in 1 Thes. iv. 1, v. 12, but his following words are not an adjuration as AV suggests. *By the coming* is better rendered

[1] On this whole section the admirable treatment in *The Pauline Eschatology*, Geerhardus Vos, Michigan, 1953 should be consulted.

'concerning the coming', for the Greek *huper*, although used in adjurations in early Greek, is not found in such a sense in later Greek, including the New Testament. *Huper* combines the ideas of 'concerning' and 'on behalf of'. It is something like 'in the interests of the truth concerning. . . .' The solemnity of the subject is heightened by the use of the full, formal title, *our Lord Jesus Christ*. For *coming (parousia)* see notes on 1 Thes. ii. 19. From the point of view of believers a most important part of the events associated with the great day is their meeting with their Lord (1 Thes. iv. 16f.). This is the aspect which is brought out in *our gathering together unto him* (cf. Mt. xxiv. 31). The noun *episunagōgē* is used elsewhere in the New Testament only in Heb. x. 25, where it signifies the gathering together of the Christians for worship.

2. Paul wishes his friends to be settled in mind, given neither to being thrown off their equilibrium by any sudden shock, nor to manifesting a habitual condition of agitation and uncertainty (cf. Eph. iv. 14 and similar exhortations to stability). The verb *saleuō, be shaken*, properly applies to the motion produced by wind and wave, and indicates a restless tossing, as of a ship not securely moored or even shaken loose from its moorings. Paul does not want them to be shaken 'from the mind' (so the Greek; not *in mind* as AV). The mind, *nous*, stands for the mental aspect of man; but it is the mind considered as the reason, the whole mental balance of the man, rather than simply the mechanism of thought. The aorist infinitive points to the idea of a sudden shock, throwing them off balance. So also *tacheōs, soon*, does not mean here a short time from now, so much as 'hastily'; 'Don't be hastily thrown off your balance' is the thought.

Or be troubled (throeisthai) is a change to the present infinitive and denotes a continuing state of agitation (cf. its use in Mk. xiii. 7). Whereas the previous expression directed attention rather to the initial shock, this has reference to the state of remaining upset.

There are three things which might bring about this

undesirable state of affairs. Some commentators have understood the words *as from us* to apply only to *letter*, the last of the three, but it seems better to take it as referring to all that precedes. *Spirit* is to be understood of some supernatural revelation. The meaning of the expression, then, is that the Thessalonians are not to be disturbed by any report that a revelation had been made to Paul to the effect that 'the day of the Lord' (so the best manuscripts) has come, or that he has said this in a sermon or written it in a letter. He totally dissociates himself from any such report.

The question arises whether *letter* refers to 1 Thessalonians or to some other letter. We should notice the reserve with which Paul writes. The expression *as from us* (*hōs di' hēmōn*) is rather vague, and one gets the impression that Paul either was not quite sure what had happened or did not care to define it too closely. The resultant expression could be taken in more ways than one. It might mean a mistaken interpretation placed on 1 Thessalonians or some other letter he had written. It might refer to a forgery put out in Paul's name (though this seems unlikely because the apostle could so easily disown it to the church), or to people saying that they had received a letter from Paul in which he had made the statement. Amid these uncertainties what is beyond any dispute is that Paul vehemently denies that he has done anything to give currency to such a report.

According to AV the statement which Paul is denying is that *the day of Christ is at hand*. This, however, is unlikely to be the meaning, since Paul himself could say 'The Lord is at hand' (Phil. iv. 5; cf. Rom. xiii. 12). What he does denounce is a report that he had said that 'the day of the Lord has already come'. The verb is *enestēken*, the perfect of *enistēmi* used as a present. It is commonly used in the New Testament to mean 'to be present', as in Rom. viii. 38, 1 Cor. iii. 22, where on each occasion it is contrasted with a verb denoting futurity. Obviously the Lord had not returned visibly in the manner outlined in 1 Thes. iv. 16f. But 'the day of the Lord' was a complex idea and it included many events. The report would mean that this series of events had begun to unfold, so that the exciting culmination would certainly appear within a very short time.

(b) The great rebellion (ii. 3-12)

(i) The man of lawlessness (ii. 3-10a). But the Thessalonians must not be deceived, whether by the kind of thing that Paul has suggested or by anything else whatever (*by any means*). The construction is broken in the following clause, but AV is right in supplying the words *that day shall not come*. The passage is animated (one imagines that the amanuensis may have found taking it down far from easy!), and the meaning so clear that the words could be omitted without danger of misunderstanding.

The necessary prelude to the coming of Christ is 'the rebellion'. The AV translation is defective at two points here: it does not give the definite article, and *falling away* hardly gives the force of *apostasia*. The article stamps the rebellion as something that was known to the readers, and evidently it had formed part of Paul's previous teaching. Our difficulty is that we have not the advantage the Thessalonians had in this matter. In classical Greek the word *apostasia* denoted a political or military rebellion; but in the Greek Old Testament we find it used of rebellion against God (e.g. Jos. xxii. 22), and this becomes the accepted Biblical usage. Paul's thought is that in the last times there will be an outstanding manifestation of the powers of evil arrayed against God. Cf. Mt. xxiv. 10ff.; 1 Tim. iv. 1-3; 2 Tim. iii. 1-9, iv. 3f. (does Rev. xii. 7ff. refer to the same kind of events?). It is as though Satan were throwing all his forces into one last despairing effort.

A feature of the rebellion will be the appearance of the *man of sin*. He will be *revealed*, which points to his existence before his manifestation (cf. i. 7 for the revelation of Christ); but it does not necessarily mean, as some commentators think, that he must have been in existence when Paul was writing. There is a textual problem here; the better manuscripts seem to favour 'man of lawlessness'. But there is no great difference between this and *man of sin*, for, as 1 Jn. iii. 4 tells us, 'sin is lawlessness' (RV). The essence of sin on the Biblical view is not its ethical quality, but the fact that it is rebellion against God. It is the assertion of the will of man instead of submission to the will of God.

It is difficult to say just who this 'man of lawlessness' is, and many suggestions have been made. Throughout history there have been numbers who have done Satan's evil work (cf. the *many antichrists* of 1 Jn. ii. 18); and this is a warning against over-hasty identification of the individual so described with any particular historical personage. From time to time we must expect that outstandingly evil men will appear. Paul's concern, however, is not with them, but with the most infamous of all, who will appear in the last days. He does not use the term Antichrist, but it is Antichrist that he has in mind; and this being will not be revealed until the end is near. He is not Satan, for he is distinguished from him (verse 9); but he is Satan's instrument, imbued with Satan's spirit.

He is described as *the son of perdition*. This is an example of the Hebraizing genitive (cf. 1 Sa. xx. 31 mg.), and it means 'he that is doomed to destruction'. Similarly it is written of that other 'son of perdition' Judas Iscariot (Jn. xvii. 12), that he fell 'that he might go to his own place' (Acts i. 25).

4. There are coincidences of language in this description with a number of passages in Daniel, notably Dn. vii. 25, viii. 9ff., xi. 36ff.; but it must not be thought that Paul is simply reproducing the thought of Daniel. Since his mind was steeped in the language of the Old Testament he naturally made use of it on such an occasion as this, but his aim is to describe a different figure, the leader of the forces of evil in the last time.

Who opposeth is a participle, and might well be rendered 'the opposer' or 'the adversary', a term sometimes applied to Satan (e.g. 1 Tim. v. 14); indeed the Hebrew *satan* means 'adversary'. The word emphasizes the kinship of the 'man of lawlessness' with his master. Closely joined with this is a second participle (there is but one article in the Greek), 'the exalter of himself'. The verb in question, *huperairō*, is found in the New Testament elsewhere only in 2 Cor. xii. 7, where, significantly, it is twice translated 'exalted above measure'. *All that is called God* seems wide enough, including as it does, the true God and any so-called god; but it is further extended by the following *or that is worshipped*, the term *sebasma* embracing all kinds of objects of veneration, such as shrines, images, altars, etc.

Next the 'man of lawlessness' is pictured as sitting in the temple and claiming divine honours. Some have understood this to refer to the setting up of an image within the shrine, and have instanced Caligula's attempt to do just this. This is not impossible; but the language indicates rather that he will sit in the holy place in person. We are reminded of the words of our Lord in Mk. xiii. 14, where the masculine participle which is used shows that a person is meant. It is clear that an important feature of the resurgence of evil in the last days will be the attempt to dethrone God. *Shewing himself that he is God. Apodeiknumi*, which is the verb employed here, is used in late Greek in the sense of 'proclaim', a sense adopted here, rightly it would seem, in many translations (e.g. Moffatt, RSV, Phillips, Rutherford). He sits in the shrine and proclaims that he is God.

5. These things were not new to the Thessalonians, for they had formed part of the original preaching. The imperfect tense *elegon* may have the meaning 'I used to tell you', or as Rutherford puts it, 'I often spoke of this'. Paul had evidently spoken much of the second coming in his original preaching, and he expected the Thessalonians to recognize his allusions accordingly. It is interesting to notice that here he uses the first person singular, instinctively recalling his personal contribution to the preaching.

6. *And now* may be logical, simply marking a transition, as in Acts iii. 17 and elsewhere; or it may be strictly temporal, in which case it will mean 'and as concerns the present', being in contrast with *in his time*. Probably the second alternative is to be preferred.

Ye know what withholdeth, says Paul; and we do well to bear in mind that the Thessalonians did know and we do not. Because they knew, Paul could content himself with an allusion; and because he did so we can only guess at his meaning. The words *what withholdeth* represent the neuter participle of *katechō,* a verb which can mean (a) 'to hold fast' (as in 1 Thes. v. 21 of holding fast the good), (b) 'to hold back' (as in Phm. 13), or (c) 'to hold sway' (if intransitive). Most commentators prefer the second sense here, but we really do not know.

Assuming that 'withhold' is the meaning, Paul is saying that the appearance of the 'man of lawlessness' is impossible at present, for there is a restraining power. This power is referred to as neuter, i.e. as a thing; but in the next verse *he who now letteth* is the masculine participle of the same verb, i.e. the power is regarded as a person. This combination of masculine and neuter inclines most commentators to see a reference to the Roman Empire which might be referred to in terms of itself, or in terms of the Emperor who personified it. Support for this comes from the generally friendly attitude of St. Paul to the Roman government, and the possibility of applying the words to certain historical circumstances: for example Claudius might be the restraining power who held back the appearance of Nero, the 'man of lawlessness', until he was taken out of the way by his death. This particular historical allusion bristles with difficulties (there is no evidence that Paul foresaw that Nero, who was only a boy when this letter was written, would turn out as he did). To interpret it as a more general allusion to the Roman Empire is also difficult for those who hold that Paul was writing under the inspiration of the Holy Spirit, for the appearance of the 'man of lawlessness' seems to take place soon after the removal of the restraining power (verse 8). Yet the Roman Empire has long since passed away, and the Antichrist has still to put in his appearance.

It is better to see in the restraining power a reference to the principle of law and government which was illustrated in the Roman Empire, but which still continues in other states. Indeed Roman law is to a large extent perpetuated in the legal systems of the states which have succeeded the Empire. The Jewish Law is another illustration of the principle, restraining the operation of sin (Gal. iii. 19, 24); and others could be given. A principle can be personified, and thus the change from the neuter to the masculine presents little difficulty. In line with this is the fact that the masculine participle may refer to a whole class rather than to an individual, e.g. in Eph. iv. 28.

Or again, there may be an allusion to some angelic being familiar in contemporary eschatological speculations. This solution attracts many and may be right; but we cannot know whether it is or not. Other commentators have suggested Satan, but this interpretation is surely excluded by verse 7 where the removal of the restraining power is the signal for the appearance of the 'man of lawlessness'. Warfield thought of the Jewish State,[1] but it is hard to reconcile this with the attitude to the Jews shown in 1 Thes. ii. 14–16. Some have suggested the Father, or the Holy Spirit, but it is difficult to see in what sense either could *be taken out of the way* (verse 7). Dibelius thought it was something somewhere, but Paul was not quite sure what, and thus shifted from neuter to masculine.

But the plain fact is that we do not know, and it seems best honestly to admit the fact, and not to try to force the passage into conformity with some particular theory which has been evolved on the basis of imperfect knowledge.

The reference to his being revealed *in his time* shows us that God is thought of as in complete charge of the whole process. When his time has come, and not till then, the 'man of lawlessness' will make his appearance; and Paul clearly thinks of the time as being in the Father's hand.

7. AV, with its rendering *the mystery of iniquity*, obscures the connection between this verse and the 'man of lawlessness'. It is better to render 'the mystery of lawlessness' with RV and RSV. The characteristic work of the lawless one is to oppose

[1]*Biblical and Theological Studies*, Philadelphia, 1952, p. 473.

the things of God, and this force of evil is already at work in the world. But it cannot reach its consummation until the restraining power is taken out of the way. The thought is like that in 1 Jn. ii. 18.

Mustērion in the Bible does not mean a 'mystery' in our sense of the term, but a secret which man can never fathom, and which can be known only by revelation. Usually it is implied that it has been revealed, so that it is now an open secret, at least among the initiates. See for example its use in Mk. iv. 11, Rom. xvi. 25, Col. i. 26, and notice the interesting phrases 'the mystery of the faith' (1 Tim. iii. 9) and 'the mystery of godliness' (1 Tim. iii. 16). The word is in an emphatic position here, the meaning being 'Revealed, I say, rather than called into existence; for in fact the evil is already working, though in secret' (Lightfoot).

8. *And then* (*tote*) seems to indicate that these further events will follow more or less immediately upon the removal of the restraining power. It is a pity that AV translates words from the same root by *that man of sin* (verse 3), *the mystery of iniquity* (verse 7), and *that Wicked* (here). We would see the continuity if we translated 'the man of lawlessness', 'the mystery of law-lessness' and 'the lawless one'. The 'lawless one' is, of course, identical with the 'man of lawlessness'. Here for the third time he is said to be *revealed*, emphasis being thus placed on the supernatural aspect of his appearing.

But Paul's primary aim is not to gratify curiosity about this being, and he gives no details of his activity. Immediately after his appearance Paul deals with his destruction. Through-out this whole section there is the underlying note of God's unchallenged sovereignty; thus the revelation of the 'lawless one' can lead only to his destruction by God. The manner of this destruction is described in words reminiscent of Isaiah xi. 4. The better manuscripts seem to read 'slay' (*anelei*) for consume (*analōsei*), but the difference is not great. *The spirit of his mouth*, better 'the breath of his mouth', is an expression occurring only here in the New Testament. It emphasizes the ease with which the Lord will destroy the 'lawless one', terrible though he will be.

Parallel to this is the concluding expression *and shall destroy with the brightness of his coming*. For the Lord even to show Himself will be sufficient to destroy the enemy. *Destroy* translates *katargēsei*, a verb which basically means 'to make idle', and thus 'to render inoperative'. It does not mean that the 'lawless one' is annihilated, but that he is made completely powerless. The word rendered *brightness* is *epiphaneia*, which means much the same as *coming* (*parousia*). Indeed in all the other five places where it occurs in the New Testament it refers to our Lord's coming, once to the first advent (2 Tim. i. 10), and four times to the second advent (1 Tim. vi. 14; 2 Tim. iv. 1, 8; Tit. ii. 13). It often appears to include the idea of splendour, and thus Rutherford here renders 'by the glory of his Presence' and Phillips 'the radiance of the coming'.

9. Just as the Lord has His coming, so the 'lawless one' has his coming. Many commentators from the earliest times have pointed out how the 'man of lawlessness' will at many points counterfeit the Christ. He will be working in the power of Satan as Christ was of God, and he will perform miracles of various kinds as did the Lord. *The working* (*energeia*) differs from *power* (*dunamis*) in that the latter denotes power simply while the former means power in action. The first part of the verse tells us, then, that the 'man of lawlessness' will embody the power of Satan.

There is some difficulty about the second part of the verse, but it seems best to take *all* as referring to all three of the following nouns, and the same applies to the final *lying* (the Greek order is 'in all power and signs and wonders of lying'). We have here three words used to denote miracles, the first referring to the power that is operative in them, the second to their characteristic as being meaningful (they point to something), and the third to the effect they have on spectators as being portents, things which cannot be explained. And all three, says the apostle, are saturated with falsehood.

10a. The thought of the previous verse is continued. *Deceivableness* should be 'deceit', and the following genitive gives its origin. The 'lawless one' will work by the method of deceit, and this proceeds from the unrighteousness which is characteristic of him (*adikia* is unrighteousness in its widest aspect; it includes all forms of evil). The range of this deceit is indicated in the participle *tois apollumenois*, 'them that are perishing' (as in 1 Cor. i. 18). The use of the present is very vivid. Paul sees the process going on before his eyes.

(ii) The man of lawlessness' followers (ii. 10b–12). In the middle of verse 10 attention is switched to those who are so misguided as to follow this deceiver. The reason for their perishing is that they *received not the love of the truth. Received* implies welcome (see note on 1 Thes. ii. 13); these men have no welcome for the gospel. *The love of the truth* (which is stronger than simply 'the truth') is an unusual expression, found only here in the Greek Bible, and it is placed in an emphatic position. We must understand *truth* not as an abstract moral quality, but rather as the truth of the gospel, the truth which is revealed by God and which comes from God (cf. Rom. i. 25). This is clear from the last part of the verse where we see that acceptance of the truth in question leads to salvation. Paul is thus giving strong expression to the idea that these people received some knowledge of God's way, but they would have none of it. They gave it no welcome. They gave it no love. And this in spite of the fact that the truth was the only way whereby they might have been saved.

11. The great Biblical truth that God is sovereign, and that His hand is to be seen in all that happens is brought out in this verse in a way which is rather startling to modern Western man, for the delusion is ascribed not to Satan but to God. This is in line with the teaching of the Old Testament, where, for example, we find it said that God put a lying spirit into the mouths of the false prophets (1 Ki. xxii. 23, and cf. Ezk. xiv. 9), and where the same action can be ascribed to Satan (1 Ch. xxi. 1) and to God (2 Sa. xxiv. 1). In Hebrew thought the powers of evil are allowed no independent existence, but are always dependent on God. As God is One who makes the wrath of man to praise Him (Ps. lxxvi. 10), His purposes are being worked out even in the evil that men (or Satan) do. In particular, God uses the evil consequences of sin as part of the punishment of the sinner. Thus in Romans i, the consequences of men's sin are not viewed as the result of the operation of an impersonal process, but three times it is said that 'God gave them up' to the consequences in question (verses 24, 26, 28). God's hand is in the process whereby the sinner receives the fitting recompense of his sin.

So here Paul sees it as due to God that those who reject the gospel come to believe a lie. *For this cause* refers us back to the preceding verse and the statement that those concerned had refused to receive the love of the truth. It is the law of life that those who take this step go further and further astray into error. The word *God* is in an emphatic position, emphasizing that what follows is not mere chance or natural law, but the result of the divine action. The true reading is 'sends' not *shall send*. Since the time of the action is clearly future this must be taken as the prophetic present, giving us the note of greater certainty. *Energeian planēs*, rendered *strong delusion*, is an expression difficult to translate. As we saw on verse 9, *energeia* denotes power in action, so that the expression indicates not merely a passive acquiescence in wrong-doing, but an active forwarding of evil. It is a solemn thought that when men begin by rejecting the good they inevitably end by forwarding evil.

The upshot of this is seen in the final statement *that they should believe a lie* (there is an article here; it is really 'the lie'). The lie is over against the truth in verse 10, and stands for that which Satan would have men believe, more particularly with regard to the 'lawless one'. This is *the* lie. But men who reject the gospel of God are bound to end by accepting evil as true. Thereby God uses Satan as the means of punishing them.

12. This purpose of God is further defined in a second clause of purpose depending on the first, *that (hina) they all* *might be damned* (lit. 'judged'). God brings such men to condemnation by way of their acceptance of the lie. They may well think that their acceptance of the lie is the end of the story (most men do not see beyond the sin that they are enjoying); but it is not. It leads necessarily in the purposes of God to condemnation.

Those who come into this judgment are *all . . . who believed not the truth, but had pleasure in unrighteousness.* Paul frequently uses the verb 'to believe', but the construction he employs here (followed by the dative) is found in his writings elsewhere only in quotations. The more usual construction throughout the New Testament (*eis* with the accusative) signifies to put one's trust in, whereas that employed here conveys the idea of giving credence to. The people referred to did not accept as true the truth of God in the gospel.

More than that. These people rejoiced in iniquity. The picture we get is of men who have rejected the light that God has given them and turned their back on the love of the truth. This cannot be done without consequences, and the particular result which claims attention is that they become immersed in their lower pursuits and come to the position where they take delight in them. So far have they become perverted from their true end (defined for us in *The Shorter Catechism* as 'to glorify God, and to enjoy him for ever') that, instead of enjoying God, they enjoy sin.

IV. THANKSGIVING AND ENCOURAGEMENT
(ii. 13–17)

(a) Thanksgiving (ii. 13–15)

13. From the contemplation of the 'lawless one' and the doom awaiting his followers Paul turns, with some relief, to the bright future which, by contrast, awaits his Thessalonian friends. In words reminiscent of i. 3 he emphasizes the obligation that rests upon him and his companions to give thanks continually for what has been wrought in and for the converts. The word order here, with its stress on obligation, may be an intentional recalling of the language of the opening of the Epistle, and a re-emphasizing of the point, made there, that any modest disclaimer made by the Thessalonians that they were not worthy of the praise bestowed on them in the first Epistle was out of place. The apostles simply *had* to give thanks for the very real work of God which was manifest in these humble believers.

He speaks of them as *brethren beloved of the Lord* (cf. 1 Thes. i. 4), where *Lord* refers to Jesus. Paul is fond of referring to Christ by this term, and it is specially appropriate here where he has been thinking of the might of Antichrist. Those *beloved of the Lord* have nothing to fear even from such a one. Notice that in this verse all three Persons of the Trinity are mentioned, as is the case also in Mt. xxviii. 19; 1 Cor. xii. 4–6; 2 Cor. xiii. 14; Eph. iv. 4–6; 1 Pet. i. 2; Jude 20f.

The matter for thanksgiving is the election of the Thessalonians and Paul makes use of an unusual word for *chosen* (*heilato*). It is used in the Greek Old Testament of the choosing of Israel in Dt. xxvi. 18 (and in a compounded form in Dt. vii. 6f., x. 15), but it is not used elsewhere in the New Testament in this sense. A number of words are employed to express the idea of election; and this may indicate that it is a deep and many-sided concept. The Thessalonians are said to have been chosen *from the beginning*, which some commentators (e.g. Findlay) understand as the beginning of the preaching of the gospel in Thessalonica. This precise expression does not occur elsewhere in Paul; but its other New Testament occurrences point us back to the beginning of all things (e.g. Mt. xix. 4; 1 Jn. ii. 13), and the idea of an election which took place before the world is familiar in the Pauline writings (cf. Eph. i. 4). Thus it seems best to take this as the sense here. There is a variant reading *aparchēn* ('first fruits') for *ap' archēs* ('from the beginning'), and this is adopted by some, e.g. Moffatt, but the evidence for *ap' archēs* seems sufficient.

The purpose of election is given as *salvation*, and this is further defined as *through sanctification of the Spirit and belief of the truth*. The first phrase points us to the complete setting apart of the whole man for the service of God, something which can be accomplished only in the power of the Holy Spirit of God (cf. I Thes. i. 5). The second is concerned rather with the response of faith to the preaching of the gospel (understanding *truth* as in verses 10, 12). The combination brings before us the primary function of the Holy Spirit, and the necessity for man's response.

14. In the previous verse Paul has thought of *salvation* as being purposed in the mind of God *from the beginning*. Now he comes to the manifestation of that purpose in time, *he called you*, and he looks forward to the future consummation in *the glory of our Lord Jesus Christ*. Cf. Rom. viii. 29, 30. Notice the characteristic emphasis on the divine call. In the Pauline writings the use of the term 'call' implies that the call has been answered. In the Gospels the terminology is different, a distinction being made between the 'called' and the 'chosen'. But though the terminology is different, the essential idea is not, and the primacy of the divine is just as clear there as here. Cf. I Thes. ii. 12, v. 24. For *our gospel* see notes on I Thes. i. 5.

The latter part of the verse does not represent something additional to *salvation* (verse 13), something to which salvation leads, but is an explanation of its content. For *obtaining* see notes on I Thes. v. 9. The glory of Christ is in view in all the gospel; further, when men receive the gospel, they become sharers in His glory (cf. Jn. xvii. 22; Rom. viii. 17). That glory has already been manifested in part (Jn. i. 14, xiii. 31) but its fullness is yet to appear (cf. i. 10, where see note).

Denney speaks of these last two verses as 'a system of theology in miniature', a statement justified by the richness of their content. There are important aspects of the Christian message which are not mentioned, such as the cross and the resurrection, but they are implied in what is said. And for men subject to the difficulties and perplexities of the Thessalonians what is said must have been extremely satisfying.

15. *Therefore*, since God has so clearly included you in His great purpose, and since that purpose cannot be overthrown even by such as Satan and the Antichrist, *brethren* (note the affectionate address in this serious exhortation), *stand fast*, and neither be frightened by the magnitude of the opposition, nor be unsettled by uncertainties about the details of the end. Paul is appealing to the verities of the Christian gospel as a safeguard against being stampeded by the kind of thing that had upset his friends.

In the second part of his exhortation, *hold the traditions*, the last word, *paradoseis*, directs attention to the derivative nature of the gospel in the spirit of 1 Cor. xi. 23, xv. 3. It stands for all Christian teaching, be it oral or written. The essential thing is that it is something handed on by one to another, but received in the first place from God. As Lightfoot says, 'The prominent idea of *paradosis* is that of an authority external to the teacher himself.' Milligan points out that the word is used in the inscriptions of 'Treasure Lists and Inventories . . . the articles enumerated being "handed over" '. This is another way of putting the truth, insisted upon in 1 Thes. ii. 13 and elsewhere, that the gospel is not of human origin, and the preacher is not at liberty to substitute his own thoughts for that which he has received.

The *traditions*, Paul proceeds, include what the Thessalonian had been taught *whether by word, or our epistle*. It does not matter in which form the word of God was delivered. Either way it was authoritative. The most probable way of understanding *epistle* is as a reference to 1 Thessalonians.

(b) Prayer for the converts (ii. 16, 17)

16. As in the first Epistle Paul brings the main section of the letter to a close with a prayer for the Thessalonians (see 1 Thes. iii. 11ff.) and some of the wording is markedly similar. So also is the language in which he introduces the concluding parts of the two Epistles.

He places *our Lord Jesus Christ himself* before *God, even our Father*, probably because the Lord Jesus has been much in mind in the preceding section. Paul's usual habit is to mention the Father first, but the order is reversed in the well-known 'grace' of 2 Cor. xiii. 14. The fact that the Lord Jesus is so closely associated with the Father, and on occasion is placed first is evidence of the way Paul thought of Him. He clearly was not sharply distinguished from the Father, and this impression is strengthened here by the fact that the verbs *comfort* and *stablish* of the next verse are both singular though there is the double subject. Paul thought of the Father and the Son as one (see also notes on 1 Thes. iii. 11).

After *God, even our Father* there are two participles linked with a common article which probably refer to the Father only, although it is grammatically possible that they refer also to the Son in spite of the fact that they are singular. Both are in the aorist, and this seems to indicate that *which hath loved us* refers to the manifestation of God's love on Calvary, and *that hath given us everlasting consolation . . .* refers likewise to the initial gift. *Consolation* is the translation of *paraklēsin*, a word which denotes more than the English term since it includes the notion of strengthening (see note on 1 Thes. iii. 2 for the verb from this root). The adjective underlines the thought that this good gift of God cannot be shaken by anything that will happen now or through eternity. Notice the characteristic stress on *hope*, for which the pagan religions of the day found little place, but which rings through the New Testament. *Good hope* means a hope that is good both in its own nature and in its results. Much that goes by the name in modern times would be disqualified on both counts; but we must never forget that the Scriptural view of hope is of something which is a certainty because it is always grounded in the divine nature and the divine promises. So here it is linked with *grace*. A hope based on God's grace can never be disappointed.

17. For the significance of the singular verbs see the notes on the previous verse. *Comfort* means rather 'strengthen', a notion which is attached also to *stablish*. Both words were used in 1 Thes. iii. 2, where see notes. Paul prays for a comprehensive strengthening of his converts, *every good word and work* including all things, great or small.

V. THE FAITHFULNESS OF GOD (iii. 1-5)

(a) Request for prayer (iii. 1, 2)

1. *Finally* (*to loipon*) brings us to the concluding part of the letter (see note on 1 Thes. iv. 1). This does not mean that there is no important topic remaining, for Paul could and did discuss weighty matters, even after such an expression; but he does imply that he has concluded his main argument. Here it immediately leads to a request for prayer (as in 1 Thes. v. 25). A minor problem arises because the verb *pray* is in an emphatic position, and is in the present, which means 'Pray continually'. Perhaps they had let Paul know that they were praying for him and his companions, and he responds with emphasis, 'Keep on praying (as you are doing)'. Or he may mean, 'Not only hold fast our teachings (ii. 15), but also pray for us'.

Have free course is literally 'may run', and it brings before us a picture of the word of the Lord as active and vigorous, moving swiftly to accomplish the divine purpose. The idea goes back to Ps. cxlvii. 15 (cf. also Ps. xix), and Paul may also have in mind his oft-repeated illustration of the Greek games. 'May run' refers to what the word does in itself, while *be glorified* is concerned rather with its effect on people. When they see what the word of God is able to accomplish within men they will glorify it as did the Gentiles in Pisidian Antioch (Acts xiii. 48). There is no *it is* in the Greek, and *even as with you* is very general. It may look back to the time of the mission, or it may refer to the time of writing, or it may include both. In the light of 1 Thes. i. 5ff., ii. 1, 13, it is probable that there is some reference to the early days in Thessalonica. Paul was clearly having difficulties in Corinth, and he recalls with nostalgia the effect of his preaching in Thessalonica. There indeed the word of God had not been bound (cf. 2 Tim. ii. 9), and Paul longs to see its swift and powerful action in Corinth too.

2. The second part of the prayer is for deliverance for the preachers (for *delivered* see notes on 1 Thes. i. 10). There is an article with *unreasonable and wicked men,* so that Paul has in mind a definite group of people, and not adversaries of the gospel in general. The aorist tense of the verb also favours a definite situation. There can be no doubt that these people were the Jews who gave the apostle such trouble in Corinth as elsewhere (see Acts xviii. 12ff.). *Unreasonable* is not a good translation of *atopōn.* The word by derivation means 'that which is out of place', and so comes to mean 'improper', 'wicked'. In late Greek it usually has this ethical connotation. This is the only place in the New Testament where it is applied to persons: the reference is to things in Lk. xxiii. 41; Acts xxv. 5, xxviii. 6. The word which accompanies it here, *wicked,* denotes not simply a passive acquiescence in badness, but an active evil. So Paul wishes his friends to pray for him to be delivered from wicked men who would oppose the gospel and harm its ambassadors.

There is a divergence of opinion as to what Paul means by *all men have not faith,* for *pistis* is ambiguous. It may mean 'faith' in the sense of belief and trust, or, with the article, 'the faith', the body of Christian teaching. Or again the word may mean 'faithfulness', 'fidelity'. Where the word applies to God it always has this last meaning; but it is doubtful whether it ever has this sense when used in the New Testament of men. Here the word has the article and our choice will lie between 'not all men exercise faith' and 'not all men accept the Christian faith'. There is not a great deal of difference between them and, whichever interpretation we adopt, Paul is clearly stressing that his opponents come from among those to whom the great Christian verities mean nothing. In view of the next verse it is probable that AV is right, for *faith* leads more naturally to what follows than does 'the faith'.

(b) God's faithfulness (iii. 3–5)

3. From the unbelief of men Paul turns to the faithfulness of God. The first word of this verse, *pistos,* like the last word of the previous verse, *pistis* (which probably suggested it), has more than one meaning. It may signify 'believing' in the sense of exercising faith, or 'faithful' in the sense of 'reliable'. Here it is clear enough that Paul is reminding his friends of the faithfulness of God (cf. 2 Tim. ii. 13; for a play on words similar to that in this passage see Rom. iii. 3).

He does not say, as we would have expected from the preceding, 'who will stablish us', but 'who will stablish you'. Paul's deepest concern was for his flock, and insensibly he passes over from his need to theirs. For *stablish*, *stērizō*, see note on 1 Thes. iii. 2, and notice the certainty with which Paul looks for this strengthening, grounded as it is on the divine nature. *Keep* is really 'guard' (*phulassō*), and adds something to what he has just said. God will not establish them and leave them. He will guard His people continually.

Evil is ambiguous, for the word could be either masculine or neuter. If the former, then the meaning is 'Guard you from the Evil One'; if the latter 'from the evil thing'. There is a similar ambiguity in the petition in the Lord's Prayer. Two points indicate that it is masculine here. First, this is by far the more common use in the New Testament; secondly, in the context, a reference to a person seems more likely than to a principle. In the last chapter Satan and his dupes have been in mind, and in the previous verse Paul has been speaking of evil men. Everything points to a person here, and we conclude that Paul is saying, 'God will guard you from all assaults of Satan'.

4. Again we have an expression which can be understood in more ways than one. It is possible to take *confidence* with *the Lord*, as AV, or with *you*, as, for example, Moffatt does, 'we rely on you in the Lord'. However there is no fundamental difference in meaning for, in any event, Paul is resting his confidence on the Lord, and saying that this gives him confidence also in the Thessalonians. Because of the faithfulness of the Lord, who perfects that which He begins in those who trust Him (see Phil. i. 6), Paul knows that he can rely on the Thessalonians. His confidence is in a performance, both present and future, of the things he commands (for this verb see note on

1 Thes. iv. 11). The question arises as to what these things are, especially in view of the fact that the section seems to lead on from verse 1, where he has been laying on them the obligation to pray for the missionaries. But much more probably he is leading up to the commands of verses 6ff. (notice the repetition of the verb *command* in verse 6).

5. Paul's confidence in God leads him into one of those short prayers so characteristic of him. *The Lord* is Jesus, as throughout this section. *Kateuthunō*, translated *direct*, means 'to make straight', and was used in 1 Thes. iii. 11 of removing obstacles out of the way. It has the idea of opening up the path so that there will be no hindrance in attaining the desired object. Paul's prayer is that Christ will open up the way for the whole of the inner life of the Thessalonians (for *heart* see notes on 1 Thes. ii. 4, iii. 13) to be concentrated on the love and stedfastness of which he proceeds to speak.

It is not clear whether we should understand the genitives in the concluding part of the verse as subjective or objective, that is, whether we should take *the love of God* to mean our love for God or His love for us, and so with *the patient waiting for Christ*. Paul's customary use would lead us to understand 'God's love for us'; but it is difficult to see how this fits into this prayer if it be understood rigidly. The expression, however, is not precise, and it may well be that Paul intends it to be taken comprehensively (so Lightfoot), including both the idea of the great love of God for us and the aspiration that this love may induce in us a corresponding love for Him.

A similar way of understanding the concluding part of the verse is probable, but *patient waiting* is not the meaning of *hupomonē*. It is the word rendered *patience* in 1 Thes. i. 3 (where see note), and it means 'the characteristic of a man who is unswerved from his deliberate purpose and his loyalty to faith and piety by even the greatest trials and sufferings' (Grimm-Thayer). Paul is then reminding them of the stedfast endurance exemplified in the life of the Master, and praying that they, in their measure, will reproduce it.

VI. GODLY DISCIPLINE (iii. 6–15)

(a) The disorderly (iii. 6–13)

The importance of this section may be gauged from the fact that, next to that on the second coming, it is the longest section in this Epistle. If we compare the treatment of this subject in the first Epistle (1 Thes. v. 14) with what we have here it is obvious that the problem has greatly intensified.

6. Paul's treatment is very authoritative; there is something of a military air about this opening verse. His word for *command* is often used of a general ordering his troops, and *disorderly* refers to the failure of a soldier to keep in rank (see note on *unruly* in 1 Thes. v. 14). The command is *in the name of our Lord Jesus which makes* it as authoritative as it can possibly be. Yet, with all this authoritative tone, there is the affectionate *brethren*, a term which Paul does not hesitate to apply also to the offenders. They are to be dealt with; but they remain brethren. Here we have the warm affection of a friend, and not the cold rule of an autocrat.

Paul enjoins them to *withdraw* from such. The verb *stellesthai* was used earlier in its history for such activities as furling sails. It signifies the withdrawing into oneself, a holding oneself aloof from the offender in question. This is not to be done in a spirit of superiority. The appeal to brotherliness shows that it is part of a man's duty to the brotherhood that he should not condone the deeds of any who, while claiming the name of brother, nevertheless denies by his actions what the brotherhood stands for.

The adverb *disorderly* is cognate with the adjective rendered *unruly* in 1 Thes. v. 14 and, as we saw in the note there, this word-group denotes the particular disorder of loafing. This is something that Paul had warned them about in person, for he reminds them that such conduct was *not after the tradition* (see note on ii. 15). There is a textual problem at the end of the verse. We can read either 'which you received', or 'which they received' (AV *which he received* has very little support); but the meaning is much the same in either case. Paul is directing their minds to the fact that he had spoken on this matter in his original proclamation.

7. All this is anything but new to them, and Paul appeals to their undoubted knowledge of their duty. In the first Epistle he has had no hesitation in speaking of the example that he and his companions had set (1 Thes. i. 6, ii. 3ff.); but here he goes further, saying that they *ought* (*dei*) to follow that example. *Dei* is more than 'it is fitting' and denotes a compelling necessity. So too, *to follow us* is really 'to imitate us'. Paul might have said 'how you ought to walk so as to imitate us' (cf. 1 Thes. iv. 1), but the shorter expression is more crisp and emphatic.

The verb translated *we behaved not ourselves disorderly* (*ētaktēsamen*) is found only here in the New Testament; but we have noted other words from the same root in the last verse and in 1 Thes. v. 14. As in those passages, the meaning is not general, but 'we were no loafers' (Rutherford). It is failure to earn one's living that Paul is thinking of.

8. The thought is continued. The expression 'to eat bread' is a Hebraism, and it extends its meaning from that of having a meal to that of getting maintenance (cf. 2 Sa. ix. 7). Paul is not saying simply that he did not have free meals, but that he refused to impose on anyone for his livelihood (cf. 1 Thes. ii. 9). This whole verse is very similar to 1 Thes. ii. 9, though his motive in making the statement is different. There he was professing the purity of his motives, while here he is appealing to the force of his example. Frame points out that, whereas Paul might have said that he had worked to set them an example, he increases the effect of his appeal by pointing out two things, first that his labour among them had been hard, constant and purely in their interests, and secondly that he had had the right to maintenance by them, but had not exercised that right.

9. *Power* in this verse is *exousia*, a word which originally meant freedom to do as one pleases, and came to mean authority or right. Milligan cites examples of its use in the papyri in wills and contracts in the sense of legal 'right'. Paul is

insisting that as a preacher, he had the full right to be maintained, an attitude which he takes up in other places. His
ideas on this subject are most fully developed in 1 Cor. ix. 3–14,
where he bases the right to maintenance on a command of the
Lord. Though more than once Paul forebore to exercise this
right he never forgot that he had it.

This right was waived in order that the preachers might
set their converts as an example. There is some emphasis on
the condescension involved, for he says literally 'that we might
give ourselves' where he might have said (as Rutherford
actually renders) 'that you might have in us a pattern'.
Ourselves is in an emphatic position, too. For *ensample* see note
on 1 Thes. i. 7.

10. *For even;* better, 'for also'. Not only did we give you an
example when we were with you, Paul says, but we also gave
you a rule in concise form. *This we commanded you* translates the
same authoritative verb as in verses 4, 6; here it is used in the
imperfect with the meaning 'This we used to command you'.
Paul is referring to a constant theme of teaching, and not to
an isolated saying. He gives the saying in the form originally
used, *hoti* (*that*) being probably the *hoti recitative,* equivalent to
our inverted commas, 'If any man won't work, neither let him
eat!' There has been much speculation as to the source of the
saying. Findlay (C.G.T.) says it is 'a Jewish proverb, based
upon Gen. iii. 19' (cf. the passages cited by Strack-Billerbeck). Deissmann thinks it 'a bit of good old workshop morality,
a maxim applied no doubt hundreds of times by industrious
workmen as they forbade a lazy apprentice to sit down to
dinner'.[1] Some see in it a Greek saying, and others try to trace
it to a saying of our Lord (cf. His own example, Mk. vi. 3).
But, while it is the kind of saying that might have arisen anywhere, in point of fact we cannot find it prior to this passage,
and it may well be that Paul himself coined it. What is clear is
that we owe to Paul the fact that it has been given a religious
sanction, and imported into the Christian scheme of things.

[1] *Light from the Ancient East,* London, 1927, p. 314.

Would is the rendering of *thelei*, and gives the impression of the activity of the will, 'If any man won't work . . .'

11. The reason for writing in this strain now appears. Paul was not indulging in generalities, but had specific instances in mind, though he mentions no names. *We hear* may mean 'we keep on hearing', or it may be more or less equivalent to the perfect 'we have heard'. *Among you* (*en humin*) is used by Paul, rather than 'of you', and his word order is 'some which walk among you', not 'some among you walk'. This form of expression may be meant to indicate that their relations to the local church were not what they should be. Paul has used the same expression in verse 7 with reference to the presence of the preachers, who, of course, did not belong to the Thessalonian church.

The report reaching him was that these folk were *disorderly* (the same word as in verse 6, where see note). Paul's play on words at the end of this verse is brought out by Moffatt's 'busybodies instead of busy'. The verb *periergazomai* (*are busybodies*) is found only here in the New Testament, but the corresponding adjective *periergos* is found in 1 Tim. v. 13 in a context which brings out plainly the meaning of the term. The idea that the second advent was near seems to have convinced them that it was useless to work for their living; and, not content with being idle themselves, they were busying themselves in the attempt to make others idle also, probably urging them to give themselves over to nothing but preparing for the great event. Such conduct is castigated.

12. Paul turns from addressing the church in general to the idlers whose conduct had provoked this whole section. He does not adopt a high and mighty tone, but speaks tactfully, as to brothers. Thus he does not address them personally ('you idlers'), but uses an impersonal form of address, *them that are such*. He adds *exhort* (*parakaleō*; see note on 1 Thes. iii. 2) to the authoritative *command* which he has employed in verses 6, 10. His exhortation is 'in' (not *by*) *our Lord Jesus Christ*, at one and the same time reminding them of the brotherly relationship they bore and of the high standards that were obligatory upon them.

Of the three points in his exhortation, *with quietness* refers to an inner tranquillity in contrast to their present excited state; *they work* to the necessity for some real labour on their part in line with Paul's own practice (verse 8); and *eat their own bread* to the whole matter of earning their living. There may be some emphasis on *their own*, for these people had been in the habit of eating other people's.

13. *But ye, brethren* turns the exhortation away from the loafers and directs it toward the whole church. Whatever the idlers choose to do, the duty of all is plain. It is quite possible that the conduct of those who had ceased to work had so annoyed the rest that they had grown irritable, and had acted otherwise than charity would direct. But the words are sufficiently general to be applicable even apart from such a specific cause.

The verb *enkakeō* has as original meaning 'to behave badly in', and thence comes to mean 'to be weary', 'to flag'. Paul uses it a number of times. *Well doing* is the participle of the compound verb *kalopoieō* which is found only here in the New Testament, though the two parts of the compound are found several times, notably in Galatians vi. 9 where the thought is much the same as here. It signifies in Milligan's phrase ' "doing the fair, the noble thing" rather than "conferring benefits" '; this latter phrase would be *agathopoieō*. Milligan further thinks that *kalos* 'carries with it the thought not only of what is right in itself . . . but of what is *perceived* to be right'. The sentence then is an exhortation to direct one's conduct to the highest ends, and that without flagging.

(b) The disobedient (iii. 14, 15)

Paul evidently thinks it likely that some of the more obstinate will not obey his directions in this matter, so he adds a few words to deal with the resulting stiuation, though he makes them broad enough to cover all that he has said, and not just the matter of idleness.

14. The word *obey*, *hupakouei*, properly applies to one who, in the position of a doorkeeper, comes to listen (cf. its use in Acts xii. 13, where it is rendered *hearken*). It carries the idea of hearing, and then of acting on what is heard. *This epistle* is a correct explanation of the Greek 'the epistle', though we should note that there have been some who connect this with the following words to give the meaning 'If any does not obey our word, designate him by letter', i.e. write to Paul about him. This interpretation has little to commend it; the word order is against it, and also the use of the definite article which, at the close of a letter, often denotes the letter just written (e.g. see 1 Thes. v. 27; Rom. xvi. 22, etc).

Note that man says Paul. His verb, *sēmeioō*, was originally neutral, but came to have a flavour of disapproval of the person or thing marked, as it does here. Among the grammarians it came to be equivalent to our *nota bene* (see Moulton-Milligan), so that it was more than a cursory notice that is meant. Paul does not say how the man is to be marked out, and this must therefore be left to conjecture.

The treatment of such a man is to withdraw from close fellowship with him. *Sunanamignusthai* is a double compound with 'the first preposition *sun* denoting "combination", the second *ana* "interchange"' (Lightfoot). It literally means 'Don't mix yourselves up with him'. This very expressive word gives the idea of familiar intercourse which is thus prohibited in the case of the erring brother. This is not as stringent a course as that advocated in 1 Cor. v. 9–11 (the only other passage in the New Testament where this verb is used), for there it is added that one is not to eat with the offender in question. Here it is only the exercise of familiar intercourse that is restrained. Plau is insisting that the erring one be regarded as a brother and treated in such a way as to bring him to his senses. So he adds *that he may be ashamed*.

15. This attitude of tenderness is insisted upon in the explicit statement that the man is still to be regarded as a brother. Probably we should take *kai* to mean 'and', rather than *yet* as AV (which takes *kai* as equivalent to *kaitoi*). Paul is not bringing out a contrasting thought, but continuing and amplifying what he has said. The order of his words is interesting. 'And admonish' is his sequence of thought, but he puts the words which exclude the offender from the category of 'enemy' before the words about admonishing him. It may be that he had some fear that the more zealous would be too eager for drastic action. At any rate he makes it clear that such a man is still to be regarded as one of themselves. He has erred, and his sin must be brought home to him; but the treatment prescribed is to be carried out entirely in a spirit of love, with a tender concern for the welfare of the man being disciplined. It is his reclamation and not the purging of the flock that is primarily in mind. For *admonish* see notes on 1 Thes. v. 12. In addition to what was said there about the sense of blame for wrongdoing attached to the word, we might add that, in Paul's hands, it seems to have the thought of an act basically friendly in the spirit of Proverbs xxvii. 6. See for example 1 Cor. iv. 14.

VII. CONCLUSION (iii. 16–18)

16. As in the first Epistle the writer proceeds to remind his readers that what he has been enjoining is not something to be achieved in merely human strength (see 1 Thes. v. 23). The emphatic *autos de* with which the verse opens turns their thoughts away from their own efforts to *the Lord . . . himself.* Paul usually refers to 'the God of peace' (see passages listed under 1 Thes. v. 23), but he generally means Christ when he uses the term 'the Lord'. On the whole it is likely that it is Christ that he has in mind here, though, as we have seen in other places, he does not sharply differentiate between God and Christ.

For *peace* see note on 1 Thes. i. 1. It is a comprehensive term for the prosperity of the whole man; this is what Paul seeks from Christ for his friends. Its supernatural origin is indicated by its association with the Lord. True peace in the deepest sense is something that man can never acquire by his own effort, but it comes as a free gift from God.

'At all times' of RV, RSV and Phillips, is no improvement on the *always* of AV as a translation of *dia pantos* (being rather the rendering of *pantote*). The idea is of a peace which remains constant and unbroken no matter what the trials. 'Continually' (Moffatt) is the sense of it. It is accompanied by *by all means* which does refer to variety in circumstances. The peace for which the apostle prays is one which will constantly remain, and which will not vary however much outward circumstances and conditions may alter.

The Lord be with you is not a different prayer altogether. The peace which the Christian enjoys is not something that has existence in its own right, but is something which is possible only because of the presence of the Lord. It is because we know that the Lord is with us, and that He will never forsake those whose trust is in Him (cf. Heb. xiii. 5) that our peace remains unshaken (Jn. xiv. 27). The Christian's peace *is* the presence of the Lord.

There may well be significance in the *all* with which the verse ends. Paul prays for them all, the dissident brethren as well as the loyal and obedient.

17. As Paul comes to the end of the letter he takes the pen himself to append a personal greeting. AV does not seem to be quite right in connecting *of Paul* directly with *salutation*, the better rendering being 'The greeting by the hand of me Paul'. The point is that Paul's custom appears to have been to dictate the letter to an amanuensis who wrote it down. Then at some point near the end he took the pen and added a few words in his own distinctive handwriting. The point at which he did this varied. For example, in Galatians he wrote several verses (Gal. vi. 11, RV), and he may himself have penned the whole of a short letter, such as that to Philemon (Phm. 19). But usually it would seem to be very near the end, and he draws our attention to the fact in 1 Cor. xvi. 21; Col. iv. 18 as well as here. The fact that he says nothing about it in other letters does not mean that he did not do it, but only that he did not emphasize it. Deissmann gives us a facsimile of a letter dated

A.D. 50 from a certain Mystarion in which the body of the letter is by one hand and the final greeting and date by another, clearly that of Mystarion himself.[1] There is nothing to draw attention to it. And in view of the fact that Paul says this is his practice we must accept what he says.

The *token* is the sign by which the letter can be recognized as genuine. The word is cognate with a verb which may be used for signing a letter and, whether this connection is in mind or not, it is the authentication that is meant. He adds *so I write* to show that it is his habit. *In every epistle* seems to show that he wrote other letters which have been lost.

It may be that there is special significance in thus calling attention to the genuineness of this letter. It does not mean that this is the first letter he has written to the Thessalonians, as some suggest. It would be natural to write in this way after he had already penned 1 Thessalonians if some doubt had arisen as to how they could be sure that a letter really did come from Paul. From ii. 2 it would seem that a situation had arisen in which a letter had purported to come from Paul, and thus the *token* was certainly needed.

18. The conclusion to this letter is identical with that to the first Epistle except that he adds the significant *all*. We have already marked Paul's tenderness towards those who were disorderly. Right to the very end he retains this characteristic, and uses a farewell which includes them with the others.

As in the case of the first Epistle *Amen* and the subscription are lacking in the best manuscripts, and are to be omitted as no part of the original.

[1]*Op. cit.*, pp. 170ff.